# Dad's Eye View

# DAD'S

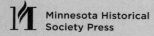
Minnesota Historical
Society Press

# Eye View

**52** Family Adventures
in the
**TWIN CITIES**

Michael Hartford

www.mhspress.org

The Minnesota Historical Society Press is a member of the Association of American University Presses.

10   9   8   7   6   5   4   3   2   1

♾ The paper used in this publication meets the minimum requirements of the American National Standard for Information Sciences—Permanence for Printed Library Materials, ANSI Z39.48-1984.

International Standard Book Number
ISBN: 978-0-87351-818-5 (paper)

Library of Congress Cataloging-in-Publication Data
Hartford, Michael, 1969–
    Dad's eye view : 52 family adventures in the Twin Cities /
    Michael Hartford.
        p. cm.
    Includes index.
    ISBN 978-0-87351-818-5 (pbk. : alk. paper)
        1. Minneapolis (Minn.)—Guidebooks.
        2. Saint Paul (Minn.)—Guidebooks.
        3. Family recreation—Minnesota—Minneapolis—Guidebooks.
        4. Family recreation—Minnesota—Saint Paul—Guidebooks.
        5. Children—Travel—Minnesota—Minneapolis—Guidebooks.
        6. Children—Travel—Minnesota—Saint Paul—Guidebooks. I. Title.
F614.M6H37 2011
977.6'5790454—dc22
                                                                        2011004447

# Contents

Map    viii

Introduction: What's the Dad's Eye View?    1

## SPRING

1. In the Heart of the Beast MayDay Parade    6
2. Minnesota Zoo    8
3. Dowling Community Garden    10
4. Minneapolis Central Library    12
5. St. Paul Central Library    14
6. Pavek Museum of Broadcasting    16
7. Prospect Park Water Tower    18
8. Milwaukee Avenue    20
9. Minnesota Children's Museum    22
10. Science Museum of Minnesota    24
11. Big Back Yard    26
12. Minnehaha Falls    28
13. Farmers Markets    30

## SUMMER

14. Chain of Lakes    34
15. Mill City Museum    36
16. Steamboat *Minnehaha*    38
17. Como Town Amusement Park    40

18. Gold Medal Park    42

19. Stone Arch Bridge    44

20. St. Paul Saints Baseball    46

21. Lock and Dam No. 1    48

22. Midtown Greenway    50

23. Minnesota History Center    52

24. 9 Nights of Music    54

25. Jim Lupient Water Park    56

26. Minnesota State Fair    58

## FALL

27. Walker Art Center and Minneapolis
    Sculpture Garden    62

28. Clifton E. French Regional Park    64

29. Foshay Tower    66

30. Hmongtown Marketplace    68

31. Midtown Global Market    70

32. Como Park Zoo    72

33. Highland Park Water Tower    74

34. Mississippi River Visitor Center
    and Walking Tour    76

35. Mississippi Gorge Regional Park    78

36. Washburn Park Water Tower    80

37. Twin City Model Railroad Museum    82

38. Choo Choo Bob's Train Store    84

39. Jackson Street Roundhouse    86

# WINTER

40. Holidazzle Parade    90
41. Minnesota Center for Book Arts    92
42. Bakken Museum    94
43. Sledding at Minnehaha Creek    96
44. Skiing at Hyland and Buck Hill    98
45. Minnesota State Capitol    100
46. Bell Museum of Natural History    102
47. Rice Park    104
48. St. Paul Winter Carnival    106
49. Snowshoeing at Mississippi Gorge
    Regional Park    108
50. Skating in the Parks    110
51. Conservatory at Como Park    112
52. Minneapolis Institute of Arts    114

Index    117

# Twin Cities
## Family Adventures

Minneapolis

St. Louis Park

Windom Park

Logan Park

Beltrami

Downtown

Midtown Greenway

Edina

Lake Calhoun

Lake Harriet

Lake Hiawatha

Lake Nokomis

# Locations

1. In the Heart of the Beast MayDay Parade
2. Minnesota Zoo*
3. Dowling Community Garden
4. Minneapolis Central Library
5. St. Paul Central Library
6. Pavek Museum of Broadcasting
7. Prospect Park Water Tower
8. Milwaukee Avenue
9. Minnesota Children's Museum
10. Science Museum of Minnesota
11. Big Back Yard
12. Minnehaha Falls
13. Farmers Markets
14. Chain of Lakes
15. Mill City Museum
16. Steamboat *Minnehaha*\*
17. Como Town Amusement Park
18. Gold Medal Park
19. Stone Arch Bridge
20. St. Paul Saints Baseball
21. Lock and Dam No. 1
22. Midtown Greenway
23. Minnesota History Center
24. 9 Nights of Music
25. Jim Lupient Water Park
26. Minnesota State Fair
27. Walker Art Center and Minneapolis Sculpture Garden
28. Clifton E. French Regional Park
29. Foshay Tower
30. Hmongtown Marketplace

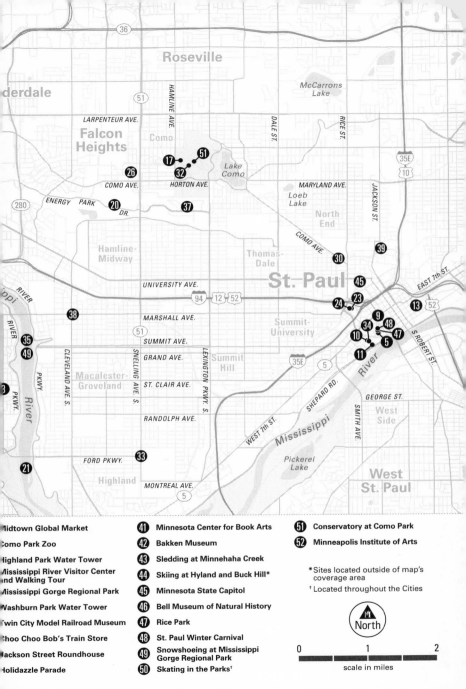

36

Roseville

derdale

51

Hamline Ave.

McCarrons Lake

Larpenteur Ave.

Falcon Heights

Como

Dale St.

Rice St.

26

Como Ave.

17    51
   32
Horton Ave.

Lake Como

Maryland Ave.

Loeb Lake

North End

Jackson St.

35E
10

280

Energy Park Dr.

20

37

Hamline-Midway

Como Ave.

Thomas-Dale

39

30

University Ave.

94  12  52

St. Paul

45

East 7th St.

38

Marshall Ave.

51

Summit Ave.

River

River

35

49

Cleveland Ave. S.

Snelling Ave. S.

Grand Ave.

Summit-University

24   23

34   9   48
10         47
         5
11

13   52

S. Robert St.

Pkwy.

River

Macalester-Groveland

St. Clair Ave.

Lexington Pkwy. S.

Summit Hill

35E   5

River

George St.

Smith Ave.

West Side

3

Pkwy.

Randolph Ave.

West 7th St.

Shepard Rd.

Mississippi

33

Ford Pkwy.

Highland

Montreal Ave.

5

Pickerel Lake

West St. Paul

21

Midtown Global Market

Como Park Zoo

Highland Park Water Tower

Mississippi River Visitor Center and Walking Tour

Mississippi Gorge Regional Park

Washburn Park Water Tower

Twin City Model Railroad Museum

Choo Choo Bob's Train Store

Jackson Street Roundhouse

Holidazzle Parade

**41** Minnesota Center for Book Arts

**42** Bakken Museum

**43** Sledding at Minnehaha Creek

**44** Skiing at Hyland and Buck Hill*

**45** Minnesota State Capitol

**46** Bell Museum of Natural History

**47** Rice Park

**48** St. Paul Winter Carnival

**49** Snowshoeing at Mississippi Gorge Regional Park

**50** Skating in the Parks†

**51** Conservatory at Como Park

**52** Minneapolis Institute of Arts

*Sites located outside of map's coverage area

†Located throughout the Cities

North

0          1          2

scale in miles

# Introduction

## WHAT'S THE DAD'S EYE VIEW?

The dad's eye view is a little above and behind the kids' eye view. As a dad, you're above, so you can scan the horizon for danger and excitement. You're also behind, because adventures are best led by the kids. A dad brings practical skills, a little planning, and a few snacks. Kids add the amazement that turns a trip into an exploit.

A good outing should include surprises not only for the kids but also for the dad. Sure, it can be gratifying to have all of the answers and dole out information to minds hungry for knowledge. But it's more fun to go into an adventure without knowing everything. As expedition leader, you don't need to be an expert on the terra incognita. You need only a rough map that points out where the dragons might lurk and where the bathrooms are. The details can be filled in along the way.

I learned this approach to family adventures from my own parents. As an army brat, I moved eleven times before I graduated from high school. Every new place was an opportunity to explore. When we lived in Germany, we would drive out to the towns beyond Aschaffenburg and Würzburg, not stopping until we could no longer see the green American license plates issued to military families. We discovered ruined castles, medieval squares, and village fairs. Could we have found these places if we'd stuck to the guidebooks? Maybe. But finding them ourselves made them all the more fun. Sometimes we got lost and had misadventures, but every outing resulted in a story, another piece of family legend that improved with each retelling.

My wife Kelly and I have a more settled life in the Twin Cities. Our twin sons Jack and Peter are nine years old and have gone to the same school with the same friends for five years now. This kind of childhood is truly strange to me. But settled doesn't mean boring, especially in the Twin Cities, where there are so many adventures to take and treasures to unearth.

*Dad's Eye View* covers many of my family's favorite Twin Cities spots. Some are well known, like the Science Museum of Minnesota, the Como Park Zoo, and the Minneapolis Sculpture Garden. Others are off the beaten path, like Milwaukee Avenue and the Washburn Park Water Tower. All of them are now part of *our* family legend.

What follows is an idiosyncratic list. It reflects my family's interests in history and literature, and in science and engineering. Another dad would certainly come up with a different list, tailored to his family's enthusiasms. But *Dad's Eye View* isn't meant to be comprehensive. Rather, it's a sketchbook of suggestions. The goal is to inspire you to go out and explore the Twin Cities with your family. Consider these places as waypoints leading to bigger and better adventures.

The world is wide, with many undiscovered countries. There are countless adventures to be had tucked away in places you might overlook if you don't take the dad's eye view.

## About the Photos

I became interested in toy and vintage film cameras in 2001, when I stumbled across a loose tangle of blogs featuring photos made with Holga and Diana toy cameras. The images were strange and dreamlike, defiantly blurry in this age of digital clarity. The cameras were essentially cheap plastic boxes offering little control over things like focus and shutter speed. To me that sounded good, like something I could learn how to do without having to read a fat manual on digital image formats and special sensor modes.

It turns out I was right. I have since collected and used quite a few, including the standard 120-format Holga toy camera, cheaply made Soviet copies of high-end Western cameras like the FED and the Lubitel, and quirky oddities like the Bosley Model C and the British Purma Special. Each camera is unique, with its own strengths and weaknesses. When I select one to take with me on a family adventure, I feel a bit like a cut-rate James Bond, surveying a range of fascinating tools offered by Q and knowing none of them will work quite as expected.

There are benefits to using these film cameras with kids. When I use a digital camera, Jack and Peter always stop what they're doing to look at themselves on the display. But with a film camera, they just keep doing what they're doing. They've learned that they won't see the images until much later. I have to finish a roll, develop the film, dry it, and then scan the pictures. The process can take as little as a day or as long as several weeks, depending on what's happening in our household.

With film images being more expensive and difficult to process than digital ones, I'm much more frugal with my picture-taking. The result is that I spend more time engaged in the activity at hand and less time documenting every moment. The pictures I do get, some of which are in *Dad's Eye View,* are more about the atmosphere and emotions of our latest adventure than its details. Like memories, the photos are a little fuzzy and open to new interpretations each time we revisit them.

# Spring

# 1

# In the Heart of the Beast
# MayDay Parade

1500 East Lake Street, Minneapolis, MN 55407
612-721-2535 • www.hobt.org

**PRICE**: Free (donations accepted)

**QUICK TIPS**: To avoid parade crowds, snag a spot north of Lake Street on Bloomington Avenue; to avoid traffic, use the Midtown Greenway bicycle trail (p. 50) or Metro Transit bus route 21

**RESTROOMS**: Try the Midtown Global Market (p. 70), Mercado Central (1515 East Lake Street), or the Powderhorn Park facilities before the parade arrives

**FAMILY TALK**: Why is there a parade in May? What are the costumes made of?

**WATCHING A PARADE IS FUN,** but being in a parade is better. When that parade is the In the Heart of the Beast MayDay Parade, the fun meter goes off the charts. The biggest event of the year in the Powderhorn Park neighborhood of Minneapolis, the parade combines political theater, a celebration of spring, and a craft bonanza.

During the month leading up to the parade, In the Heart of the Beast Puppet and Mask Theatre turns its space into a chaotic mad scientist's laboratory, where cardboard boxes, papier-mâché, and paint are transformed into tigers, dragons, skeletons, and flowers. The theater holds public brainstorming sessions to set the parade's tone and story each year. Then the artists who run the parade workshops give participants latitude in imagining their costumes and props.

On parade day, the story—always topical, often political, and usually whimsical—unfolds behind funky hand-painted banners along Bloomington Avenue, from just north of Lake Street to Powderhorn Park. The enthusiasm the event inspires is infectious, and by the end, it's hard to tell who is marching and who is watching: this parade demands audience participation.

The rest of the year, In the Heart of the Beast Puppet and Mask Theatre presents full-length plays and kids' matinees, usually involving workshops and hands-on activities. Like the annual parade, these performances break down barriers between actors and audiences, between on stage and backstage. After their first winter matinees there, Jack and Peter built their own rickety theater, made puppets from cardboard and paper bags, and performed nightly plays. More proof that theater is empowering; it's the story, not the special effects, that makes for a great show.

**MAKE A DAY OF IT:** Stick around after the parade for the spring ceremony, when the sun is carried across Powderhorn Lake on fanciful boats. Grab a bite to eat on Lake Street at the Midtown Global Market (p. 70) or Mercado Central (1515 East Lake Street #5; 612-728-5483).

# Minnesota Zoo

13000 Zoo Boulevard, Apple Valley, MN 55124
952-431-9200 • www.mnzoo.com

**PRICE:** $$$

**QUICK TIP:** Some attractions, including the farm and the Woodland Adventure play area, are open seasonally

**RESTROOMS:** Plentiful

**FAMILY TALK:** If you were a zookeeper, which animal would you want to take care of? How are zoo animals different from wild animals?

**THE MINNESOTA ZOO** sprawls across five hundred acres and includes an indoor tropical forest, an aquarium, and an IMAX theater. The zoo is home to many of the usual suspects; lions, tigers, and bears abound. But the favorite for our family is the Wells Fargo Family Farm, with chickens, rabbits, sheep, goats, pigs, cows, and horses. Especially in the spring, when new calves, foals, and piglets are on display, the farm at the zoo offers an opportunity to see animals almost as exotic to us as komodo dragons and cockatoos.

Not that komodo dragons and cockatoos aren't exciting. You just can't touch them like you can the sheep and goats. And when you visit them, you can't ride a hay wagon pulled by a tractor. The monorail through the zoo is nifty, but the tractor at the farm is far more interesting, with its loud and visible inner workings.

Of course, the farm isn't the only place at the Minnesota Zoo to touch animals: if you're daring (or foolish), you can stick your hand into a tank of small sharks at Discovery Bay. I'm always nervous as the boys pet the sharks, rehearsing my explanation to my wife for the missing digits I'm sure will result. But so far, we've left the zoo unscathed. We're probably at greater risk from the pigs, omnivores of the highest order, than from the well-fed sharks.

**MAKE A DAY OF IT:** A trip to this zoo easily fills a day, with many animals left over for future visits.

**3**

# Dowling Community Garden

46th Avenue South and 39th Street East,
Minneapolis, MN 55406
www.dowlingcommunitygarden.org

**PRICE:** Free

**QUICK TIP:** Look just east of the garden for a wide-open spot that's
great for running and rolling

**RESTROOMS:** Try the Riverview Cafe, a family-friendly spot at
3745 42nd Avenue South

**FAMILY TALK:** When should different vegetables be planted?
What kinds of animals might live in this garden?

**ONE OF THE BEST PLACES** in the Twin Cities to watch the
seasons pass is Dowling Community Garden in Minneapolis. The
collection of 190 plots was established in 1943 as a victory garden, encouraging people to grow their own food during World
War II. Today it's one of the oldest continuously cultivated community gardens in the country, and its crops are as varied as
the people who work the plots: heirloom tomatoes, sunflowers,
pumpkins, and beans fill the garden and draw not only human
visitors but also bees, butterflies, and birds.

In the spring, Dowling Community Garden, like the dozens
of other such gardens large and small scattered about the Twin
Cities, is full of activity. If you visit, you'll see people raking,

tilling, weeding, and planting. The urban landscape is wonderfully transformed by these spaces, turning the grids of streets and sidewalks into garden paths. Summer brings more activity to Dowling, along with the lush growth encouraged by a season of care. In fall, the harvest starts to thin out the tangles. And in winter, our family's favorite time to visit, the garden becomes still and mysterious, with snow drifting over the tomato beds and last year's sunflowers holding a lonely vigil. It's a good time to point out animal tracks and watch birds hopping about looking for seeds.

**MAKE A DAY OF IT:** Walk to Mother Earth Gardens at 42nd Avenue South and 38th Street East (612-724-2296); where you'll find everything you need to create your own vegetable and flower patch. Warm up with a cuppa joe or hot cocoa at Fireroast Mountain Cafe (3800 37th Avenue South; 612-724-9895).

# Minneapolis Central Library

300 Nicollet Mall, Minneapolis, MN 55401
952-847-8000 • www.hclib.org

**PRICE:** Free

**QUICK TIPS:** Take the light rail downtown to the Nicollet Mall station and skip the hunt for parking; check out the building's green roof, visible from the reading areas on the library's upper levels

**RESTROOMS:** Plentiful

**FAMILY TALK:** How many books are in this library?
Why are libraries important?

**THE MINNEAPOLIS CENTRAL LIBRARY** building, which opened in 2006, is a thoroughly modern hub. It has extensive open stacks plus a comfortable, inviting atmosphere; there are cozy chairs, quiet corners, and tons of volumes to browse. I also like being able to request books from across the region with the click of a mouse.

The library boasts kids' events almost daily, ranging from story hours to surprising treats like flamenco dancers and a film series. But by far the best features—at least according to Jack and Peter—are the elevators, complete with multimedia displays and great views of the atrium, where a statue of Minerva from the original Minneapolis Athenaeum guards the escalators. The boys never begrudge me a visit to the history stacks, though they do insist on running the elevators for each trip.

**MAKE A DAY OF IT:** Trek to the nearby Mill Ruins Park, which holds Mill City Museum (p. 36), the Guthrie Theater (818 2nd Street South; 612-377-2224), and Gold Medal Park (p. 42).

# St. Paul Central Library

90 West 4th Street, St. Paul, MN 55102
651-266-7000 • www.stpaul.lib.mn.us/locations/central.html

**PRICE:** Free

**QUICK TIP:** Check the events calendar on the library website
for the Loki Players' puppet show schedule

**RESTROOMS:** Plentiful

**FAMILY TALK:** What things besides books belong in a library?

**THE ST. PAUL CENTRAL LIBRARY** is just the sort of place I
imagine when I think of a big-city library: marble halls, winding
staircases, polished wooden shelves, and an enduring dignity.
There's a hush to the place invited not by the librarians, who
are friendly and helpful, but by the building itself, with its thick
walls and dense stacks of books.

One of the charms of this spot is the children's library,
located on the ground floor. On its walls are sketches by Robert
McCloskey: you'll easily recognize Michael the policeman from
McCloskey's *Make Way for Ducklings* and his harmonica-puffing
character Lentil. The library's puppet theater, home to the Loki
Players, is used for puppet shows and story times.

Perched on one of the shelves here is a model of the *Titanic*.
Jack and Peter are experts on this subject, having checked out
every book on the "unsinkable" ship from our neighborhood

library in Minneapolis. A quick glance at the St. Paul library catalog turned up *Titanic* books that our family had yet to explore. Hennepin County library card holders are treated like honored guests in St. Paul, so we're always able to cart some knowledge home with us.

**MAKE A DAY OF IT:** Cross the street and enjoy a picnic in Rice Park (p. 104); in warm weather, look for George's Hot Dog Stand.

# Pavek Museum of Broadcasting

3517 Raleigh Avenue, St. Louis Park, MN 55416
952-926-8198 • www.pavekmuseum.org

**PRICE:** $$

**QUICK TIP:** The staff is incredibly helpful and knowledgeable, so accept any offer they make for additional information or hands-on fun

**RESTROOMS:** Plentiful

**FAMILY TALK:** Would you rather listen to a radio or a phonograph? Why are the screens on old televisions so small when the cabinets are so big?

**THE PAVEK MUSEUM OF BROADCASTING,** tucked away in a nondescript building behind the post office in St. Louis Park, may be the coolest secret destination in the Twin Cities. Built around the collection of Joe Pavek, a former instructor at Dunwoody Institute in Minneapolis, the museum is crammed with radio- and television-related equipment dating back to the beginning of the twentieth century. It holds radios, gramophones, telegraph equipment, jukeboxes, wire and tape recorders, television cameras, and teletype machines, all in good working order.

My two-hour tour with Jack and Peter included playing a theremin (an electronic instrument featured in many sci-fi movies), competing in a quiz show, sending Morse code messages, reading news off a teletype, and producing a radio show. There's even a model of the kind of ship radio the *Titanic* had; it throws sparks and hums menacingly when it's engaged.

Everything in the Pavek Museum is bulky and inefficient by contemporary standards. Who needs a phonograph when you have an MP3 player? Why bother with Morse code when you can text? But everything in the museum is also tactile, loud, and mechanical. You and your kids can lift the lid, see the gears, and understand how it all works. The wizardry is on display, not hidden behind a smooth façade, and that's the best kind of magic.

**MAKE A DAY OF IT:** Bike along the nearby Cedar Lake Trail (parallel to County Road 25, accessible at Beltline Boulevard), or hike at Bass Lake Preserve (3515 Beltline Parkway; 952-924-2540) or Wolfe Park (3700 Monterey Drive; 952-924-2540).

# 7

# Prospect Park Water Tower

55 Malcolm Avenue Southeast, Minneapolis, MN 55414
www.minneapolisparks.org

**PRICE:** Free

**QUICK TIP:** A walk through this hilly neighborhood can be tough,
so wear your sturdy shoes and be prepared to help smaller kids

**RESTROOMS:** Try Cupcake (3338 University Avenue Southeast)
or the Overflow Espresso Café (2929 University Avenue Southeast)

**FAMILY TALK:** Why is this water tower on a tall hill?

**THE STORY THAT BOB DYLAN** was inspired by the Prospect
Park Water Tower when he wrote "All Along the Watchtower" is
probably fictional; Jimi Hendrix claimed a North African prov-
enance for the song, and surely growling wildcats are rare in
Southeast Minneapolis.

With its conical top and arched windows resembling men-
acing eyes, this structure, commonly called the Witch's Hat, is
deserving of *some* legend. It's visible from almost anyplace along
the Mississippi River north of Franklin Avenue and is a brood-
ing presence on its hill.

Once a year, the tower is open to the public, during the
neighborhood ice cream social on the Friday after Memorial
Day. The line to climb the spiral staircase to the top is long, but
it's well worth the wait: the view of the city is one of the best

you'll find. From the tower's vantage, the urban forest canopy is as impressive as the downtown skyline.

Even without scaling the tower, Prospect Park offers beautiful vistas of the city. It's a climb—the hill is the highest natural point in Minneapolis—but comfortable benches are waiting at the summit. And as evening comes on and the sun sets behind downtown, the park offers the perfect spot to spin a few tales and imagine that the tower holds secrets rather than one hundred and fifty thousand gallons of water.

**MAKE A DAY OF IT:** Eat lunch across the Franklin Avenue Bridge at True Thai (2627 East Franklin Avenue; 612-375-9942), or head to University Avenue for a sweet treat at Cupcake (3338 University Avenue Southeast; 612-378-4818).

# Milwaukee Avenue

Runs between Franklin Avenue and 24th Street East,
and 22nd and 23rd avenues, in Minneapolis
www.ci.minneapolis.mn.us

**PRICE:** Free

**QUICK TIP:** Look for the train-themed play area halfway down
the avenue, beckoning little engineers and conductors

**RESTROOMS:** Try the Second Moon Coffee Shop
(2225 East Franklin Avenue)

**FAMILY TALK:** Why are the houses here so small? Can you tell
which houses are newer?

**LOCATED JUST SOUTH** of busy Franklin Avenue, Milwaukee
Avenue is a peaceful urban oasis. Small brick houses, most built
in the early twentieth century, line the car-free street. Their open
porches are brightly painted, and in the spring and summer their
gardens are full of flowers. The pedestrian street offers a relaxing
place to stroll and a safe stretch for kids to ride their bicycles.

Milwaukee Avenue wasn't always like this. Its tidy little
houses began as temporary dwellings thrown up by railroad
companies to house immigrant workers. They had few ameni-
ties—no indoor plumbing, barely functional basements, and
poor insulation. The houses were squeezed onto a street origi-
nally zoned as an alley: until 1906, Milwaukee Avenue was

named 22½ Avenue. By the 1970s, the structures had fallen into disrepair and were slated to be razed by the city.

A local neighborhood group, the Seward West Project Area Committee, saved these two blocks with political savvy and hard work. On the eve of the planned demolition, the group got the neighborhood listed on the National Register of Historic Places, which temporarily halted the wrecking ball. They rehabilitated the houses that could be salvaged, removed the ones that couldn't, and had the street closed to traffic. In the 1980s, new houses were built on the avenue, all modeling the scale and appearance of the originals. You have to look closely to tell which houses are new and which are old.

**MAKE A DAY OF IT:** Stop by Pizza Lucé's Seward location (2200 East Franklin Avenue; 612-332-2535) just across Franklin, as well as the Seward Co-op Grocery & Deli (2823 East Franklin Avenue; 612-338-2465) a few blocks east.

# Minnesota Children's Museum

10 West 7th Street, St. Paul, MN 55102
651-225-6000 • www.mcm.org

**PRICE:** $$

**QUICK TIPS:** Take your family on the third Sunday of the month,
when Target sponsors free admission, or avoid the crowds by visiting
on a day Target doesn't sponsor

**RESTROOMS:** Plentiful

**FAMILY TALK:** Is it easier to move blocks on the conveyor belt or in
your hands? How many colors can you get from the white lights in
the shadow theater?

**THE BEST PLACE TO BE** in St. Paul on a rainy day is the giant
anthill at the Minnesota Children's Museum. Or maybe it's in
the water room there, floating Ping-Pong balls through a maze
of pipes and valves. Or perhaps it's using hand-cranked con-
veyor belts to move foam blocks up and around a pint-sized
factory that benignly mimics Charlie Chaplin's *Modern Times*.

Our family started visiting the Children's Museum before
Jack and Peter could walk. The museum has a wonderful
crawler-friendly play area with challenging, brightly colored
obstacles. We kept visiting until the boys were ready to graduate
to the Science Museum of Minnesota (p. 24). Although Jack and
Peter are convinced that the Children's Museum is far beneath

them now, they still manage to enjoy themselves when we visit for younger cousins' birthdays. Oh, the suffering of kids who are forced to race boats down a sluice and make giant soap bubbles!

The philosophy behind the Children's Museum is simple: kids learn best when they're allowed to explore on their own. It's a very tactile place, with objects to pick up, spin, splash, drop, and throw. The mysteries of the world—from machines, to water, to the grocery store—are set out at little-kid height with blanket permission to dig in and figure it out.

The only drawback to this philosophy is that it doesn't apply to the rest of the world. When the boys were still in Children's Museum mode, we made our first trip to the Science Museum. That visit almost ended in paleontological tragedy: the special exhibit of animated dinosaurs was so inviting that Jack and Peter had to be held back from climbing over the ropes to get a better look.

That's why the Children's Museum is still fun for them now: it's nice to be someplace where you can reach out and touch the fascinating stuff.

**MAKE A DAY OF IT:** Pick up fresh popcorn at Candyland, around the corner (435 Wabasha Street; 651-292-1191), or order a malt and french fries up the street at Mickey's Diner (36 West 7th Street; 651-222-5633). Even your pickiest eater will be satisfied.

# 10

# Science Museum of Minnesota

120 Kellogg Boulevard West, St. Paul, MN 55102
651-221-9444 • www.smm.org

**PRICE:** $$$

**QUICK TIP:** Consider a Science Museum membership: it pays for itself in one or two trips; grants access to permanent exhibits, movies, and special events; and brings gift shop and parking discounts

**RESTROOMS:** Plentiful

**FAMILY TALK:** How did they get that boat on the roof? Why were Ice Age animals so big?

**IF JACK AND PETER** could live anywhere in the state, maybe in the world, I suspect they would pick the Science Museum of Minnesota. They would sleep on the cushions in the Hmong house, bathe with the rubber duck in the wave simulator, and spend mornings on the lookout from the tugboat on the roof. There would be no chance of boredom. After mastering the weather machines and the microscopes, they would map earthquakes around the world.

I might, if I were lucky, be invited to visit them occasionally. I'm a big fan of the quack medical materials display. I also like to pay my respects to the mummy and marvel at the prehistoric beaver skeleton, which looks a bit like a small bear with a long tail. With my personal tour guides to show me around the epidemiology and optical illusion exhibits, I'm sure I would learn a lot.

What the kids couldn't teach me, I could probably pick up from one of the instructors in the weekend and school break classes offered through the museum. So far, we've learned about animal tracks, LEGOs, and pinball machines. It seems that just about any science topic, from dinosaurs to space travel, has been the subject of a class at the Science Museum.

The only problem with living at the museum is that you'd lose the anticipation and excitement of visiting. While never having to leave would be great, never getting to go might be a drag. And once you moved in, there'd really be no dream quite so grand left to fulfill.

**MAKE A DAY OF IT:** Explore the nearby Mississippi riverfront, Harriet Island Regional Park (200 Dr. Justus Ohage Boulevard; 651-266-6400), and Seven Corners Hardware (216 West 7th Street; 651-224-4859), the most incredible hardware store in the Twin Cities.

# 11

# Big Back Yard

120 Kellogg Boulevard West, St. Paul, MN 55102
651-221-9444 • www.smm.org/bigbackyard

**PRICE:** $$$

**QUICK TIP:** Don't skip the camera obscura: it offers a natural upside-down projection of the river

**RESTROOMS:** Plentiful inside the Science Museum of Minnesota (p. 24)

**FAMILY TALK:** Is the shape of the Mississippi River changing? How can you affect the speed of water?

**THE SCIENCE MUSEUM** of Minnesota (p. 24) is packed with exciting stuff, but when our family visits in the spring and summer, Jack and Peter rush first to the Big Back Yard. Outdoor, hands-on exhibits fill the space between the museum and the Mississippi River. Open seasonally, the Big Back Yard has a miniature golf course that makes water resource management fun and a maze made up of native prairie plants. But neither of those things is as fun as the giant sand table.

The sand table teaches about braided rivers. A fountain sends rivulets of water through the sand, causing meandering channels to form and change. You can move the sand around, forming dams and islands and canyons, and watch as the water changes its course and gradually, grain by grain, reclaims your structures. The sand table displays both permanence and change in the natural world. "You cannot step twice into the same river," Heraclitus observed some two and a half millennia ago. Indeed, the sand table is the same table every time we visit, but its rivers have shifted and become something new.

This doesn't bother the boys in the least. No matter how many times they've built rivers before, they still exert mighty efforts to engineer new waterways, calling instructions back and forth as they shape the sand to match their vision. Then, they take great pleasure in starting the flood and watching their empire tumble away.

At that moment, I think more of Ecclesiastes than Heraclitus: striving is folly; there is nothing new under the sun; all is vanity. These can be grim thoughts on a winter evening, when the snow piles up minutes after I've shoveled it, but not on a spring afternoon by the river.

**MAKE A DAY OF IT:** St. Paul Central Library (p. 14) is a quick stroll away; across the river is Lilydale Regional Park (950 Lilydale Road; 651-632-5111), home to a historic brickyard: see the remains of the kilns that produced much of the building material for old St. Paul.

# 12

# Minnehaha Falls

Minnehaha Park, 4801 South Minnehaha
Park Drive, Minneapolis, MN 55417
612-230-6400 • www.minneapolisparks.org

**PRICE:** Free

**QUICK TIPS:** Head to the base of the falls for the most spectacular
views; watch the park system website for walking tours of the area;
in the winter, there are often moonlight snowshoe hikes here

**RESTROOMS:** Located in the park pavilion

**FAMILY TALK:** Where did the falls get their name? Were the falls
always in the place they are today?

**HENRY WADSWORTH LONGFELLOW'S** epic poem *The Song
of Hiawatha* is set, in part, at Minnehaha Falls, but the poet
never visited Minnesota. He learned Algonquin tales from books
and relied on reports from travelers to the West to fill in the
poem's landscape. That hasn't stopped the city of Minneapolis
from naming streets, neighborhoods, parks, and libraries for
Longfellow and the characters in his epic poem, however.

Minnehaha Park, home to Minnehaha Falls, has been the
heart of a Minneapolis summer for more than one hundred
years. The falls, which drop water from Minnehaha Creek and
send it along to the Mississippi River, would seem attraction
enough, but there has always been much more to do here. Once

upon a time, people could take a train to the park's "Princess" Depot and visit the park's zoo and arboretum. The zoo is gone, as are the trains, but the depot remains. It's now run as a museum, complete with a telegraph and antique timetables.

In the spring, rent a bike, grab a picnic table, or listen to music. We've heard bluegrass and jug band jamborees at the band shell. At the Sea Salt Eatery (4801 Minnehaha Avenue; 612-721-8990), accordion players and jazz trios have serenaded us while we've sampled the best clam po'boy in the Twin Cities.

In winter, when the restaurant closes, the bikes are put away, and the musicians move indoors, the falls turn starkly beautiful. The tumbling water freezes into an icy sculpture, and the twisted branches of naked oaks cast strange shadows on the snow. It's a wonderful time for snowshoes and for listening to the wind. You might hear the echoes of summer's last festivities or maybe Hiawatha himself composing love songs to Minnehaha.

**MAKE A DAY OF IT:** Ride a bicycle to Fort Snelling State Park (101 Snelling Lake Road, St. Paul; 612-725-2724; the trail runs parallel to Hiawatha Avenue south from the falls) or travel east to the Wabun Picnic Area (4655 46th Street South; 612-230-6400), which holds shelters, a playground, and a wading pool with fountains.

# 13

# Farmers Markets

**Midtown Farmers Market:** 2225 East Lake Street, Minneapolis, MN 55407 • 612-724-7457
www.midtownfarmersmarket.org

**Mill City Farmers Market:** Chicago Avenue and 2nd Street South, Minneapolis, MN 55401 • 612-341-7580
www.millcityfarmersmarket.org

**Minneapolis Farmers Market:** 312 East Lyndale Avenue North, Minneapolis, MN 55405 • 612-333-1718
www.mplsfarmersmarket.com

**St. Paul Farmers' Market:** 290 East 5th Street, St. Paul, MN 55101 • 651-227-8101
www.stpaulfarmersmarket.com

**PRICE:** $

**QUICK TIPS:** Bring your own bags to make transport home easier; bring your appetite, too: most of the markets feature "street food" you won't find anyplace else

**RESTROOMS:** Portable toilets are available during the summer; try the Mill City Museum (p. 36) lobby at the Mill City market

**FAMILY TALK:** Are any of these vegetables different from the ones you would find in a store?

**MOST CITY KIDS,** counting myself and my boys, have trouble envisioning where food comes from. We've heard of mythical places called "farms," and we've seen pictures of cows and chickens. But our connection to the sources of milk, eggs, and vegetables is tenuous. It all comes from the grocery store, and big trucks are involved. Beyond that, it gets fuzzy.

Luckily, Minneapolis and St. Paul have a growing network of farmers markets. These markets may not help us understand *where* our food is from, but they help us understand who produces it. The people who bag our peas and strawberries, who hand us a block of cheese or a hunk of jerky, are the people who grew the food, and a little of their personality comes through in the meals we make with it.

The personality of the market comes through, too, and each market is a little different. The Minneapolis Farmers Market brings in people selling pineapples, oranges, and seafood, as well as local fruits and vegetables. The Midtown Farmers Market on East Lake Street, our family's favorite, has arts and crafts, fresh crepes, and local music. The St. Paul Farmers' Market bustles with local Hmong farmers selling bitter balls, greens, and peppers.

At all of the markets, the selection is seasonal, so you must time your visit just right to get the best tomatoes, peppers, and asparagus. It's worth the effort and planning, though, to taste Minnesota's fruits and vegetables at their peak.

**MAKE A DAY OF IT:** Tour Target Field (between 5th and 7th Streets North at 3rd Avenue North; 1-800-33-TWINS) after the Minneapolis Farmers Market. Following a trip to the St. Paul market, stroll through Mears Park (221 East 5th Street; 651-632-5111).

# Summer

# 14

## Chain of Lakes

3000 Calhoun Parkway, Minneapolis, MN 55408
www.minneapolisparks.org

**PRICE:** $

**QUICK TIP:** Parking lots around the lakes are metered, so come with quarters or order a parking pass from the city parks website

**RESTROOMS:** Available at the Lake Harriet (4300 East Lake Harriet Parkway) and Lake Calhoun (3000 Calhoun Parkway) park pavilions; portable toilets are stationed at most of the swimming beaches during the summer

**FAMILY TALK:** How were these lakes formed? How deep do you think they are?

**MY WIFE KELLY** wants a sailboat. She imagines us regally cruising Lake Calhoun, the perfect picture of a Minneapolis summer afternoon. My boating desires are much simpler: all I want is a canoe. A canoe gets you closer to the shoreline and lets you sneak up on turtles and frogs basking on their logs and lily pads. It's easy to steer and hard to sink, both high on my list of requirements for watercraft.

When I imagine us on a sailboat, I see myself tangled in ropes, dodging a wildly swinging boom while trying desperately not to run aground. In a canoe, I could prop my feet up and let the gentle current that connects Minneapolis's Chain of

Lakes—Cedar Lake, Lake of the Isles, Lake Calhoun, and Lake Harriet—carry me along with my lazy dreams.

I nearly have Jack and Peter convinced; they love kayaks, which are almost like canoes. When we rent a canoe at Lake Calhoun and paddle our picnic lunch across to Cedar Lake, the boys even take turns providing the power. Lately, however, they've been seduced by books about sailing, so I may lose the watercraft battle eventually. Perhaps they'll be willing to tow my canoe behind their sailboat.

**MAKE A DAY OF IT:** Ride the streetcar from Lake Harriet as far as Lake Calhoun (board at Queen Avenue South and 42nd Street West; 952-922-1096; www.trolleyride.org), visit the Bakken Museum (p. 94) on Lake Calhoun's western shore, or browse the shelves at Birchbark Books (2115 21st Street West; 612-374-4023) near Lake of the Isles.

# 15

# Mill City Museum

704 2nd Street South, Minneapolis, MN 55401
612-341-7555 • www.millcitymuseum.org

**PRICE:** $$

**QUICK TIPS:** The Flour Tower elevator ride is fun and educational, but it can be unnerving for younger kids—prepare to have one land in your lap; don't miss Kevin Kling's film *Minneapolis in 19 Minutes Flat*

**RESTROOMS:** Plentiful

**FAMILY TALK:** Why were mills built here? What grains are in the foods we eat?

**MILL CITY MUSEUM** puts to good use the ruins of the flour mills that made Minneapolis. When Washburn "A" Mill burned in 1991, the city worked with the Minnesota Historical Society to salvage the wreckage and transform it into a museum and interpretive center. Today exhibits describe the rise, fall, and resurrection of the milling district, as well as how grain becomes flour and how flour is used.

The museum's storytelling appeals not just to the eyes and ears but also to the hands. A model with toy trains, trucks, and ships helps youngsters understand how grain makes its journey from farm to mill to market. Two water tables teach the physics of dams, turbines, and logjams, and let kids play with water while they learn about the falls powering the mills. Visitors also can design a cereal box, build a puzzle map of the river, and turn a giant wood-and-metal turbine.

Our family usually visits the museum's demonstration kitchen to try out its various gadgets and, if we're lucky, sample its tasty treats. The kitchen exhibit includes a look at how Betty Crocker, the General Mills icon, has changed over the years. Always a whiz in the kitchen, Betty got a new hairdo every decade or so.

Outside the museum is Mill Ruins Park (103 Portland Avenue South; 612-313-7793), where the industrial remnants of the milling district are exposed. You can see the tailraces and sluice runs that brought the power of St. Anthony Falls to bear on the mills' turbines, and you can imagine the thunderous hum that filled the place when it was the world's milling capital.

**MAKE A DAY OF IT:** Follow the Stone Arch Bridge (p. 44) to Water Power Park (www.waterpowerpark. com), where sawmills once harnessed the power of St. Anthony Falls and where electricity is still generated.

# 16

## Steamboat *Minnehaha*

Operated by the Museum of Lake Minnetonka,
5425 Timber Lane, Excelsior, MN 55331
952-474-2115 • www.steamboatminnehaha.org
(boats depart from 400 Lake Street, Excelsior,
and 300 Lake Street East, Wayzata)

**PRICE:** $$$

**QUICK TIP:** Even on a warm day, pack a light jacket: it's much
cooler on the lake

**RESTROOMS:** Public facilities at Excelsior Commons recreation area
(Lake and Water streets); or try the Dunn Brothers at 11 Water Street

**FAMILY TALK:** What powers a steamboat?

**WE'RE USED TO** operating vehicles that have benefited from a
century of user interface design. Car dashboards are chock-full
of dials, gauges, and buttons that let us monitor every aspect
of the engine's operation. If something is off-kilter, we expect
flashing lights and humming buzzers to alert us and, if possible,
diagnose the problem.

I was surprised to find that this hasn't always been the case.
Indeed, it's possible to diagnose and fix engine problems with
nothing more than a stethoscope and an array of levers. The
engineer on the steamboat *Minnehaha* did it right before our
very eyes, moving around the engine with a stethoscope held

up to the pipes. He did it so well that he could take time out to explain his work and let the kids listen to the steam rushing through the boat's tangle of pipes.

The maroon-and-gold steamboat *Minnehaha* is a streetcar boat—essentially a floating streetcar. When it was put into service in 1906, it was part of Twin City Rapid Transit Company's streetcar line, the western end of which brought travelers to Lake Minnetonka's resorts and Big Island Amusement Park. In 1926, after the park shut down and ridership fell, the service closed. Steamboat *Minnehaha* and other similar boats were dismantled or scuttled, three of them weighted down with debris from the abandoned park. They sat at the bottom of the lake until 1980, when the *Minnehaha* was raised and a long restoration process began.

In 1996, seventy years after it sank, the *Minnehaha* began taking passengers around Lake Minnetonka again. Today visitors can cruise the lake aboard the steamboat—taking in the area's history and glimpsing the mansions scattered about its bays—and listen to the thrum of a masterfully operated engine.

**MAKE A DAY OF IT:** Visit the Excelsior Streetcar Line (3rd and George streets; 952-922-1096) and ride through town on a restored trolley. Walk along the lakeshore at Excelsior Commons (Lake and Water streets; 952-653-3673) recreation area.

# 17

# Como Town Amusement Park

1301 Midway Parkway, St. Paul, MN 55103
651-487-2121 • www.comotown.com

**PRICE:** $$

**QUICK TIPS:** Before you go, visit the park website to preview the rides and how much they cost; Hodge Podge Park, a complex of ropes, slides, and swings, is a great value for younger kids

**RESTROOMS:** Plentiful

**FAMILY TALK:** Why is it fun to go on scary rides? What makes some rides scarier than others?

**THE PROBLEM WITH** traveling funfairs is that they travel: you need to seek them out or be lucky enough to have one land nearby. Plus, they can be scary for parents, thanks to Tilt-A-Whirls that tilt a little too precariously and operators with more tattoos than teeth. Kids love the noise and implicit dangers, but dads get sweaty palms.

Como Town Amusement Park at St. Paul's Como Park manages to avoid the funfair's drawbacks. It doesn't travel, so you always know exactly where it is, even if parking can be hard to find. The rides are in perfect condition but offer all the chills of the rusty, rattling kind. And the staff is great with kids and parents alike.

With a roll of ride tickets in their pockets, Jack and Peter

can spend a summer afternoon scampering from Screamin'
Dragon Roller Coaster to Drop Zone, fueled by hot dogs and
root beer. Kelly and I can follow at a respectable distance, enjoy-
ing the fun vicariously.

That Como Town is surrounded by the other great attrac-
tions of Como Park is icing on the cupcake. When kids get bored
with the rides, there's the zoo to explore (p. 72), a miniature golf
course (our favorite stop), a garden conservatory (p. 112), and
big fields to run around in.

The Minnesota State Fair (p. 58), located not far away,
eclipses the excitement of Como Town for twelve days at summer's end, but there are many more days when Como Town is
the best ride around.

**MAKE A DAY OF IT:** In the summer, listen to live music at Como
Lakeside Pavilion (1360 Lexington Parkway North; 651-488-4920)
and rent a paddleboat to take a lazy trip around the lake.

# 18

## Gold Medal Park

900 2nd Street South, Minneapolis, MN 55415
www.ci.minneapolis.mn.us

**PRICE:** Free

**QUICK TIP:** Start a bike ride here; connect to trail systems running east or west but note that the hills are steep as you travel downriver

**RESTROOMS:** Try the Guthrie Theater lobby (818 2nd Street South) or the Minnesota Center for Book Arts (p. 92)

**FAMILY TALK:** How did this park get its name? Why is it fun to roll down hills?

**WERE SAMUEL JOHNSON,** an eighteenth-century writer and critic who loved to roll down hills, to visit modern Minneapolis, he would be delighted by Gold Medal Park. The soft green slopes of its central hill simply demand that the visitor take an exuberant tumble to the bottom. It was the first thing Jack and Peter wanted to do when they got to the top, and who was I to stop them?

Opened in 2007, Gold Medal Park is one of the newest green spaces in Minneapolis. Together with the Guthrie Theater (818 2nd Street South; 612-377-2224), Mill Ruins Park (103 Portland Avenue South; 612-313-7793), and Mill City Museum (p. 36), the park has turned this stretch of Mississippi riverfront from an industrial corridor into a showcase for history, theater, and nature.

The park is dominated by its dome-like hill. Follow the spiral path to the summit for an ideal picnic site and wonderful views of the Guthrie's steel and glass, as well as the Stone Arch Bridge (p. 44) and the Minneapolis skyline.

In spring and summer, the inviting slope of green grass beckons kids to roll willy-nilly to the bottom. (In winter, it's a tempting sledding hill.) Adults, too, may feel the call of the grass. Just keep in mind that your joints probably aren't as flexible as they once were.

**MAKE A DAY OF IT:** Across Washington Avenue, eat inside a trolley car at the Old Spaghetti Factory (233 Park Avenue; 612-341-0949) and read up on your favorite superheroes at Big Brain Comics (1027 Washington Avenue South; 612-338-4390).

# 19

# Stone Arch Bridge

Mississippi River, from Portland Avenue South and 1st Street
South, to Hennepin Island Park, 420 Main Street East,
Minneapolis, MN 55413 • www.ci.minneapolis.mn.us

**PRICE:** Free

**QUICK TIPS:** This is the place to be for Fourth of July fireworks;
arrive early to claim your spot, and take the light rail into
Minneapolis: cars are jammed up for hours after the show

**RESTROOMS:** Try the Mill City Museum lobby (p. 36) on the west
side of the river or the Nicollet Island Pavilion
(40 Power Street) on the east side of the river

**FAMILY TALK:** Why does the bridge have arches? Why was it
built here?

**WITH ITS DISTINCTIVE CURVE** and magnificent arches,
the Stone Arch Bridge is one of the great structures of the Twin
Cities. It connects downtown Minneapolis to Nicollet Island and
the city's Old Main Street neighborhood, where the village of St.
Anthony stood before it became Minneapolis. The bridge also
links Minneapolis to its history as a milling and railroad hub,
with reminders along its length of the trains loaded with grain
and flour that rolled here a century ago.

There are no more trains on the bridge; it's a bicycle and
pedestrian route now. On a bright summer day, it's a busy

thoroughfare. From the bridge, you can take in the powerful St. Anthony Falls, watch boats and barges make their way through the locks, and sometimes catch sight of eagles and hawks hovering over the abandoned bridge footings and tailraces downstream.

The Stone Arch Bridge is also one of the best people-watching spots in the Twin Cities. We've seen saffron-robed monks from the nearby Buddhist temple, couples having their wedding portraits taken, and all manner of bicyclists making their way along the bridge's curve.

**MAKE A DAY OF IT:** Take a walk down Old Main Street, stop by the stately Nicollet Island Inn (95 Merriam Street; 612-331-1800) and duck under the Hennepin Avenue Bridge on Nicollet Island to see a neighborhood of Victorian houses seemingly lost in time.

# 20

# St. Paul Saints Baseball

1771 Energy Park Drive, St. Paul, MN 55108
651-644-6659 • www.saintsbaseball.com

**PRICE:** $$

**QUICK TIP:** Check online for schedules and special events

**RESTROOMS:** Plentiful

**FAMILY TALK:** Why does the pitcher stand on a mound?
Does the ball move faster when it's thrown or when it's hit?

**BASEBALL IS AMERICA'S** pastoral pastime, a slow-paced
game for a lazy summer afternoon. Which means, unfortu-
nately, that it's not a great match for a kid's attention span:
there are long periods of boredom stretched between sudden
action, and it's all too easy for first-time ballgame visitors
to miss a double play or a home run because their focus has
wandered.

The St. Paul Saints seem to have taken this into account
when planning their park and their games. While there's plenty
of good baseball out on the field to please a fan, there are also
musicians, pig-naming contests, and audience-participation
games to break up the monotony. A nice big play area is set up
near the stands, perfectly situated so a dad can keep one eye
on the game and the other on the kids. And the concessions

at Midway Stadium are generally cheap, fast, and kid friendly: plenty of hot dogs, pizza, and ice cream.

**MAKE A DAY OF IT:** Midway Stadium is near Micawber's Books (2238 Carter Avenue; 651-646-5506), which has a great selection of kids' books, and the Twin City Model Railroad Museum (p. 82).

# 21

# Lock and Dam No. 1

5000 West River Parkway, Minneapolis, MN 55417
612-724-2971 • www.nps.gov/miss/planyourvisit/lockdam1.htm

**PRICE:** $

**QUICK TIP:** Park at Godfrey Park (5000 West River Parkway), above
the Lock and Dam entrance, where West River Parkway bends

**RESTROOMS:** Located up the stairs of the lock building, near the
walkway across the locks

**FAMILY TALK:** Why does a river need locks? What is the dam's job?
What kinds of boats travel through here?

**LOCK AND DAM NO. 1** opened in 1917 just south of the Ford
Parkway Bridge and just east of Minnehaha Falls (p. 28). Though
it wasn't the first lock and dam on the Upper Mississippi River,
as its name suggests, it did provide a navigable channel north to
St. Anthony Falls, and eventually to Coon Rapids.

Like the Highland Park Water Tower (p. 74), Lock and Dam
No. 1 is open to the public each July during Highland Fest. The
U.S. Army Corps of Engineers allows visitors into the control
room and lets kids operate the locks. Since the system is fully
automated, this consists of pressing a button and watching the
monitor display the volume of water pouring into or out of the
lock chamber. Visitors can also page through the lockmaster's

handwritten logs, which include weather, news, and river traffic notes from the lock's nearly one hundred years of operation.

Even when its offices aren't open, the lock's walkways and bridge are accessible to the public. Old hand-operated mechanisms—including a massive wheel that would surely have built up some muscles with repeated turning—decorate the walkways, with interpretive plaques explaining their use. On a summer afternoon, when barges and pleasure boats turn the Upper Mississippi into a river highway, you can watch the lock helping boaters navigate the river's slope and imagine the far-off places the waters will carry them.

**MAKE A DAY OF IT:** Explore the Mississippi Gorge Regional Park (p. 78), with trails that follow the bluffs all the way into downtown Minneapolis. Stop for ice cream at Sea Salt Eatery in Minnehaha Park (4801 Minnehaha Avenue; 612-721-8990).

# 22

## Midtown Greenway

Runs parallel to Lake Street from West River Parkway to Chowen
Avenue; entrances along the route include Brackett Park,
Minnehaha Avenue, Bloomington Avenue, Lyndale Avenue, and
Calhoun Village • 612-879-0103 • www.midtowngreenway.org

**PRICE:** Free

**QUICK TIPS:** Stop on the bridge over Hiawatha Avenue for great
views of the neighborhood; see the professionals at Freewheel Bike
Shop (2834 10th Avenue South; 612-238-4447), if your bike needs
emergency service

**RESTROOMS:** Public restrooms are available at Brackett Park
(2728 39th Avenue South), at the east end of the Greenway; also try
Freewheel Bike Shop (on the Greenway) and Midtown Global Market
(p. 70), at the halfway point; public restrooms are available at the
Lake Calhoun pavilion (3000 Calhoun Parkway) at the west end of
the Greenway

**FAMILY TALK:** What holds up the big bridge? What did this
bicycle path used to be? What should you do when someone says,
"On your left"?

**I TRAVEL BY BICYCLE** whenever I can, barring ice and rain
blowing parallel to the ground. I bike because it's cheap, efficient,
and environmentally friendly and because it's fun. Biking turns
my daily commute into an adventure. I can sail along under my
own power, living by my wits on roads that are getting friendlier

for cyclists every day. Traveling long distances with my kids by bicycle is a little more challenging. They can ride on quiet residential streets without too much trouble, but they aren't quite ready to tackle major roads. Sidewalks aren't the safest place to ride, with pedestrians, alley traffic, and other obstacles to deal with.

The solution for our family has been the Midtown Greenway bicycle path. We can get to swimming lessons at the Uptown YWCA (2808 Hennepin Avenue South; 612-874-7131), to the Chain of Lakes (p. 34), to the Midtown Global Market (p. 70), and to neighborhood parks and cafes, all without dodging cars and people.

Visiting places by bike helps Jack and Peter fill in their mental maps of the city. When you're ferried around by the Mom and Dad Taxi Service, the connections between destinations are obscured and mysterious. But when you travel under your own power, at slow speeds, you discover the links between places. Your mental map becomes detailed and rich. This is good training for kids. Whether or not they become avid cyclists, they learn how to make their way in the world.

**MAKE A DAY OF IT:** Look for signs along the Greenway that indicate what's available on street level; grab the lunch of your choice, from hot dogs to Mexican seafood, at Midtown Global Market (p. 70).

# 23

# Minnesota History Center

345 Kellogg Boulevard West, St. Paul, MN 55102
651-259-3000 • www.minnesotahistorycenter.org

**PRICE:** $$

**QUICK TIP:** Watch the History Center website for special events, including performances by costumed history players

**RESTROOMS:** Plentiful

**FAMILY TALK:** How did they get that airplane up there?

**THE MINNESOTA HISTORY CENTER** is one of the reasons I chose to live in the Twin Cities. I visited in 1992, when the building was brand new, to do research for my master's thesis. The archives were so rich and the museum so engaging, I knew I had found a place that takes its history seriously. Now I bring my family with me to the museum.

Every visit with Jack and Peter turns up something unexpected. So far, we've roamed through the rooms of a St. Paul house, experienced the wind and sirens of the 1965 Fridley tornado, and viewed Prince's purple suit and Ann Bancroft's exploration gear. We've even climbed through a grain elevator, cranked a Model T, and tried to pull a horse-drawn trolley. History, it turns out, can be exhausting.

**MAKE A DAY OF IT:** Walk up Summit Avenue to the James J. Hill House (240 Summit Avenue; 651-297-2555) and investigate how a millionaire railroad builder lived. Visit the Cathedral of St. Paul (239 Selby Avenue; 651-228-1766) on the way.

# 24

# 9 Nights of Music

Minnesota History Center
345 Kellogg Boulevard West, St. Paul, MN 55102
651-259-3000 • www.minnesotahistorycenter.org

**PRICE:** Free

**QUICK TIPS:** Check the performance schedule on the museum website; look inside for the music when the weather is bad

**RESTROOMS:** Plentiful

**FAMILY TALK:** Why are there different kinds of music and dances?

**OVER NINE EVENINGS** in July and August, the main patio of the Minnesota History Center (p. 52) pulses with music. And when good music is playing, getting out on the dance floor is hard to resist, even for kids.

Teachers from the Tapestry Folkdance Center in Minneapolis—always ready to help novices at 9 Nights of Music—have tried to teach us more complicated moves. But to enjoy dancing, we've discovered you really need only one step. A simple three-count move works for us whether the music is Vic Volare's swing, the Vibro Champs' rockabilly, or Café Accordion Orchestra's gypsy jazz. Add in the occasional turn and twirl, and you'll look almost like a pro.

Not that you even have to dance if you don't want to. The hill above the patio begs to be draped with a picnic blanket, and the music goes well with tuna salad, potato chips, and peanut butter sandwiches. Should you happen to doze off under a perfectly blue evening sky, while mariachi, jazz, or bluegrass music plays, no one will mind.

**MAKE A DAY OF IT:** Before the show, take a trip down John Ireland Boulevard to the Minnesota State Capitol (p. 100). The History Center's exhibits are also free from 5 to 8 PM on Tuesday evenings.

# 25

# Jim Lupient Water Park

1520 Johnson Street Northeast, Minneapolis, MN 55413
612-370-3989 • www.minneapolisparks.org

**PRICE:** $$

**QUICK TIPS:** Get a season pass if you plan to visit often; reserve shelters at the water park for summer birthday parties

**RESTROOMS:** Plentiful

**FAMILY TALK:** How many seconds does it take to go down the slide? How many seconds does it take to climb back up?

**PUBLIC POOLS HAVE CHANGED** a lot since I was a kid. The high dive used to be the big attraction. Passing the swimming test so you could jump off the diving board was the goal of many a summer. Having tackled that challenge, building up the courage to actually *use* your diving board privileges took the rest of the season. I never managed to dive off the top board, though I did have a couple of spectacular belly flops from it.

There are no high dives at the Jim Lupient Water Park, but that doesn't mean there aren't thrills. There are three twisting slides—one that requires an inflatable raft, and two where you're on your own. There's also a bridge of floating foam logs below the slides, for a rolling, slippery crossing.

Jack and Peter love the slides now that they've surpassed the forty-two-inch height requirement, and they keep count of how many trips they've made. Each time, they fearlessly launch themselves into the tubes and splash wildly out the bottom.

They miss out on the moment of truth that the high dive offered. They've never stood on the edge with their toes out in space, realizing that as high as it looked from below, it looks much higher from above. But they're so busy making the loop from top to bottom that they never pause to hear my "When I was a kid" lecture. They get enough of those anyway.

**MAKE A DAY OF IT:** Book a ride aboard the *Minneapolis Queen* paddleboat (952-474-8058, www.twincitiescruises.com) at Boom Island Park (724 Sibley Street Northeast; 612-230-6400) for a cruise to St. Anthony Falls and Nicollet Island.

# 26

# Minnesota State Fair

1265 Snelling Avenue North, St. Paul, MN 55108
651-228-4400 • www.mnstatefair.org

**PRICE:** $$$

**QUICK TIPS:** Before you go, plot out your campaign with a map from the fair website; bring your wallet, an empty stomach, and comfortable shoes

**RESTROOMS:** Plentiful

**FAMILY TALK:** Why are there state fairs? Who goes? What food can you get at the fair that you can't get anyplace else?

**THE MINNESOTA STATE FAIR** is about food, rides, animals, music, political candidates, live television, and more. It's an exhilarating, exhausting twelve days ending on Labor Day. It's also the traditional way to close out a Minnesota summer.

It can be overwhelming to face the crowds at places like the CHS Miracle of Birth Center and Sweet Martha's Cookies. And it can be an expensive undertaking to pay for food and fun. But I like to think of the fair as an investment in memories. This one hot day of barns and rides, milk shakes and french fries, pays dividends throughout the year.

Picking and choosing is the key. There is simply too much packed into the fairgrounds to do it all and escape with a shred of sanity. Edit your list down to the essentials and hope for serendipitous surprises along the way.

Our state fair experience must include a trip on the River Raft Ride and a visit to the DNR Building. For my wife Kelly, one must-have is frozen coffee on a stick at the Farmers Union Building, which also features great live old-time and bluegrass music. We've been happy to happen upon a friend's swing band, former teachers eating corn on the cob, and favorite local celebrities as we've made our circuit.

The fair was easier when Jack and Peter were very young and confined to the stroller. Though pushing the stroller through the crowds could be challenging, wheeling sleeping kids to the gates at the end of the day was a lot easier than forcing them to march to the exits. The boys, more mobile now, are better at digging in their heels. This is where carrots (or cookies) have worked better than sticks. Note the best treats by the gate on the way *in* and use the promise of one last taste of forbidden fruit to urge the kids *out*.

**MAKE A DAY OF IT:** Or two.

# Fall

# Walker Art Center and Minneapolis Sculpture Garden

1750 Hennepin Avenue, Minneapolis, MN 55403
612-375-7600 • www.walkerart.org

**PRICE:** $$

**QUICK TIPS:** Visit on a Thursday night or the first Saturday of the month, when Target sponsors free admission; the sculpture garden is free and open daily, 6 AM to midnight

**RESTROOMS:** Plentiful

**FAMILY TALK:** What is the cherry made of? How is art in the museum different from art in the garden?

**I APPROACHED OUR FIRST VISIT** to the Walker Art Center with more than a little trepidation. I feared a repeat of our first trip to the Science Museum of Minnesota (p. 24). Back then, little fingers accustomed to the hands-on displays at the Minnesota Children's Museum (p. 22) kept reaching out for untouchable objects and inciting the wrath of security guards. I also worried that much of the postmodern art would fly too high above the boys' heads. I had known art school students in the 1990s, and having survived my own brushes with critical theory in graduate school, I expected a lot of high-concept lingo.

Though I did have to keep a close eye on the boys' hands, I shouldn't have worried about the postmodern artwork being too advanced for them. Since they were approaching the museum without any intellectual baggage, they could see the pieces for what they were: bright, kinetic, and full of whimsy. There were televisions with animated shorts, machines that whirred and buzzed, and huge canvases with cryptic markings and broad strokes.

The Walker is still a museum, however, and Jack and Peter grew antsy after awhile with their hands in their pockets. A visit to the Minneapolis Sculpture Garden across the street was the perfect antidote. The boys could interact with art on their own terms and as their museum experience extended into the outdoors. They ran through the mirrored labyrinth, rode the Arikidea swing, and used the giant metal frame to compose views of the Basilica of St. Mary (88 7th Street North; 612-333-1381).

**MAKE A DAY OF IT:** Cross the Irene Hixon Whitney Bridge east over Hennepin Avenue to Loring Park (1382 Willow Street; 612-370-4929), which offers walking paths, flower gardens, and a playground. Grab a burger at Joe's Garage (1610 Harmon Place; 612-904-1163).

# 28

# Clifton E. French Regional Park

12605 Rockford Road, Plymouth, MN 55441
763-694-7750 • www.threeriversparks.org

**PRICE:** $

**QUICK TIP:** Bring a picture ID to check out GPS units at the visitors center and take your kids geocaching

**RESTROOMS:** Available at the park building next to the play area and at picnic areas located along the walking trails

**FAMILY TALK:** How many turtles can you see in the stream?

**GIRLS ARE DIFFERENT FROM BOYS.** I was reminded of this when I chaperoned Jack and Peter's second-grade classes on a field trip to French Regional Park. On our hike around the lake, one of the boys asked for a drink from my water bottle. I warned him that it was filled with toilet water (my ruse for keeping my water for myself). This only made it more attractive, and the story spread quickly from boy to boy until it became a minor legend. The girls were utterly scandalized and refused to be dragged down to our level.

The boys and girls weren't so different, though, when we got to the park's climbing structure. They all took to the ropes and bridges with wild whoops, bold as pirates in the rigging. I'd never seen such an impressive play structure—high and wide and inviting—nor had I seen so much daring and fun in one place. If the school playground had a structure like this one, I doubt any teacher could ever coax them down.

Our family went back to the park with some neighbors a few months later and brought our bicycles so that we could explore the trails that circle the park. They're good trails, smoothly paved, and we had a great ride. But it was short: the ropes have a powerful gravity.

**MAKE A DAY OF IT:** The Maple Grove Community Center (12951 Weaver Lake Road, Maple Grove, MN 55369; 763-494-6500), located about eight miles north of French Park, features an indoor water park, outdoor skate park, and indoor playground. Plentiful dining is available at the Rockford Road Plaza (4190 Vinewood Lane North) between the park and 494.

# Foshay Tower

821 Marquette Avenue, Minneapolis, MN 55402
612-215-3700 • www.whotels.com/minneapolis

**PRICE:** $$

**QUICK TIP:** Pack the jackets: it can be cool on the observation deck

**RESTROOMS:** Located in the museum and hotel lobby

**FAMILY TALK:** Why would someone want to build the tallest building in the city? How far can you see from the observation deck?

**AT 447 FEET, WITH 32 STORIES,** the Foshay Tower was the tallest building west of the Mississippi in 1929. The building once boasted the fastest elevator in the Twin Cities, promising a speedy ride of 37 seconds to the top floor. Foshay Tower pays homage to the Washington Monument, and its obelisk shape is unique among American skyscrapers.

Wilbur Foshay, the impresario behind the eponymous tower, had dreams that matched his skyscraper's scale. He commissioned a John Philip Sousa march for the opening gala in October 1929. The dedication of the lobby sculptures by Harriet Frishmuth included a dance by Siegfield Follies stars. The interior was decorated with imported marble and mahogany and finished with gold-plated fixtures. Foshay Tower was as excessive as any Jazz Age extravaganza, and alas, as doomed as any F. Scott Fitzgerald hero. Six weeks after the tower opened,

Wilbur Foshay's financial empire collapsed. The check to Sousa bounced, and Foshay went to prison for securities fraud.

Today the Foshay Tower is home to a swank Starwood W Hotel. The ground floor's Art Deco interior has been transformed by glass and neon into a thoroughly postmodern space, though some of the original details remain. If you brave the dim lighting, you'll find that the Foshay still has a feature none of its glass-and-steel neighbors can claim: a museum and outdoor observation deck.

Purchase your ticket at the hotel's concierge desk and ride the still-speedy elevator to the 31st floor. The museum here contains shelves of Foshay memorabilia: photographs and postcards, stationery and knickknacks, and news notices from the tower's long history. The walls are covered with maps and photographs.

A short flight of stairs leads visitors up to the observation deck. Parents and acrophobes will find the curved iron cage and high walls surrounding the deck reassuring. The gaps in the metalwork are wide enough to allow spectacular views but narrow enough to keep even small climbers safe. Telescopes at the four corners provide close-up views of the Foshay's neighbors, the Minneapolis streetscape, and the expanse of suburbs beyond downtown.

**MAKE A DAY OF IT:** Walk through the skyways into other skyscrapers. At the IDS Tower (80 8th Street South), gaze up at geometric windows in the Crystal Court. Inside the Rand Tower (527 Marquette Avenue), look for Art Deco detailing in the staircase and lobby.

# Hmongtown Marketplace

217 Como Avenue, St. Paul, MN 55103
651-487-3700 • www.hmongtownmarketplace.com

**PRICE:** $

**QUICK TIP:** Visit the food court in the West Building

**RESTROOMS:** Available in the buildings that flank the outdoor market area

**FAMILY TALK:** Where did the Hmong people come from? What things can you buy at this market that you can't buy anyplace else?

**A TICKET TO SOUTHEAST ASIA** is spendy, but a journey into the culture of the Hmong people is practically free. On Como Avenue, within sight of the Minnesota State Capitol (p. 100) and the Cathedral of St. Paul (239 Selby Avenue; 651-228-1766), is the bustling Hmongtown Marketplace, which makes Vietnam, Laos, and Thailand feel very close indeed.

The first thing I noticed about the marketplace was its symphony of sound. Traditional Hmong songs dueled with Asian pop music in stalls selling CDs and DVDs. Shopkeepers and customers haggled over prices. Young people were speaking to elders in a mix of Hmong and English. I could stand all day and listen, but there are too many sights to take in: brightly colored clothes flutter in the wind; televisions play movies I've never seen at my local theater; and the greens, browns, and reds of fresh vegetables, herbs, and spices brighten the shadows at the back of the lot.

It's a smell, however, that has fixed the marketplace in my memory. On my first visit, as I walked past the clothing stalls, a breeze carried the bright scent of cilantro and basil. It's not an unfamiliar smell, but in that dusty St. Paul lot it was magical—a fresh green bridge across oceans and time.

**MAKE A DAY OF IT:** Add a visit to the Minnesota State Capitol (p. 100) to round out the day.

# 31

# Midtown Global Market

920 East Lake Street, Minneapolis, MN 55407
612-872-4041 • www.midtownglobalmarket.org

**PRICE:** $$

**QUICK TIPS:** Don't overlook the market's specialty grocery shops when deciding where to eat; check the website for class and event schedules: chess, knitting, and dance lessons are offered frequently

**RESTROOMS:** Plentiful

**FAMILY TALK:** What did this building used to be?

**THE MIDTOWN GLOBAL MARKET,** inside the old Sears building on East Lake Street, houses more than a dozen food stands. I would eat the shrimp mole at the market's La Sirena Gorda every day if I could. For better or worse, that's not an option. My wife won't let my waistline grow to match that of "the fat mermaid" on the stand's sign. I do eat there during family outings, though, while the boys munch on hot dogs from Andy's Garage, and Kelly enjoys spring rolls from a Vietnamese restaurant nearby.

But the market is more than a place where everyone can get their favorite foods and eat at the same table. It's a community center, with gift shops and groceries, clubs, live music, and classes for kids and adults. Last winter we started meeting a neighbor and her kids on Friday evenings at the market, where

Kelly was taking a knitting class. We were awash in scarves for several months.

The building is also a great example of how to put old space to new use. Built in 1928, it was Sears Roebuck's regional catalog center and department store and a major employer in the neighborhood. The massive structure closed in 1994 and sat empty until 2006, when it reopened with the market, a hotel, corporate headquarters for a health care provider, and housing. The character of the old building has been preserved, but the marketplace has transformed it into a new kind of hub for the East Lake Street neighborhoods.

**MAKE A DAY OF IT:** Lunch here after a matinee at In the Heart of the Beast Puppet and Mask Theatre (p. 6) or during a trip along the Midtown Greenway bicycle path (p. 50).

# 32

## Como Park Zoo

1225 Estabrook Drive, St. Paul, MN 55103
651-487-8200 • www.comozooconservatory.org

**PRICE:** Free (donations encouraged)

**QUICK TIP:** Getting to the tigers and wolves is a hike from the main building but worth the effort. Fortify yourself at one of the snack stands before heading out

**RESTROOMS:** Plentiful

**FAMILY TALK:** Would any of these animals live together in the wild? Why are zoos important? Which animal would you most like to be?

**COMO PARK ZOO** started small, with some deer, elk, and buffalo. Though the zoo has added giraffes, penguins, sea lions, apes, polar bears, and more, it remains a small, almost intimate, place. Its size gives kids a chance to get to know the animals in a way that's difficult at larger zoos. It's easy to see the animals here and develop favorites that must be seen at each visit.

Our favorites, polar bears Neil and Buzz, swim back and forth with the combination of grace and awkwardness that's unique to bears. Their lazy backstrokes seem to relax them and their visitors, especially on stifling summer afternoons. Their peripatetic swims are a study in polar Zen.

By contrast, the monkeys in the primate house are all about adrenaline. They leap from branch to branch, chattering and bickering, inspiring small visitors like Jack and Peter to hop fitfully from foot to foot. I might prefer to swim with the polar bears, if I could be sure they wouldn't mistake me for a snack, but the boys would rather jump around with the tamarins.

Other animals here model different behaviors: the stately giraffes, the unflappable flamingos, the elegantly slow sloth in the Tropical Encounters exhibit. There's a creature for every mood and ample opportunity to anthropomorphize. Suggesting that the kids be less like the monkeys and more like the gorillas—stoically waiting their turn to roam through their outdoor pen—won't offer any insights into real animal behavior, but it might win parents a few minutes of quiet before the kids' urge to climb takes over again.

**MAKE A DAY OF IT:** Drive through the Como Park neighborhood to Micawber's Books (2238 Carter Avenue; 651-646-5506), or stop just beyond the park's western gates at Java Train Cafe (1341 Pascal Street North; 651-646-9179), which features a kids' menu and ice cream.

# Highland Park Water Tower

Ford Parkway and Snelling Avenue,
St. Paul, MN 55116 • www.stpaul.gov

**PRICE:** Free

**QUICK TIPS:** Watch the city website for dates when the tower is
open to the public; the view in the fall is spectacular

**RESTROOMS:** Try the SuperAmerica station across Snelling Avenue
(1580 Ford Parkway) or the Highland Park Public Library (1974 Ford
Parkway)

**FAMILY TALK:** Why are there two blue towers nearby, and why are
they shaped like globes?

**THERE ARE 151 STEPS** in the Highland Park Water Tower's
staircase, according to the materials we picked up in the lobby.
However, this was not the number Jack and Peter came up with.
That their numbers differed from each other as well as from the
official count led to a brief argument about methodology: Is the
floor you start on a step? Do the landings count? What about
the platform at the top?

I'm sure that Clarence W. Wigington, the tower's designer
and the nation's first African American municipal architect,
never considered the possibility of such a discrepancy. If he had,
he would have numbered the steps, though that would have
taken away some of the fun.

The tower is open to the public twice a year, once in July during Highland Fest, a neighborhood festival, and again in October for viewing fall color. From the tower, visitors can see downtown St. Paul, downtown Minneapolis, and the river neighborhoods of both cities.

Just as interesting as the view from the top is the view on the way up. The staircase encircles the water tower's tank, which can contain two hundred thousand gallons of water. Holding the tank's steel plates together are rivets the size of a child's head. There's no official record on the number of rivets involved, and fortunately Jack and Peter haven't tried to count them yet.

**MAKE A DAY OF IT:** Eat lunch down Ford Parkway on Cleveland Avenue at Punch Neapolitan Pizza (704 Cleveland Avenue South; 651-696-1066) or Cecils Deli (651 Cleveland Avenue South; 651-698-6276), which serves an out-of-this-world corned beef on rye.

# 34

# Mississippi River Visitor Center and Walking Tour

Lobby, Science Museum of Minnesota
120 Kellogg Boulevard West, St. Paul, MN 55102
651-293-0200 • www.nps.gov/miss

**PRICE:** Free (deposit required to borrow walking tour iPods)

**QUICK TIP:** On the walking tour, the Harriet Island pavilion is a smart pit stop: there are no more restrooms until you cross the High Bridge and are back on West 7th in downtown St. Paul

**RESTROOMS:** Also available in the museum lobby

**FAMILY TALK:** Why isn't there a waterfall here anymore? What kinds of rocks can you see?

**TUCKED AWAY IN A CORNER** of the Science Museum of Minnesota (p. 24) is the National Park Service's Mississippi River Visitor Center. It's easy to miss but deserves a stop. Read up on Acadia, Yellowstone, and the rest of the nation's nearly four hundred national parks, monuments, and visitor centers, as well as the history, geology, and culture of the Mississippi, from Itasca to New Orleans.

At the desk, ask about ranger-guided and self-guided walking tours. One takes you on 4.5-mile loop from the Science Museum, through Harriet Island Regional Park, and over the

High Bridge. On that walk, our family stood where the tallest waterfall in North America roared some ten thousand years ago from a height of more than two hundred feet. Crossing the High Bridge was somewhat disconcerting, since I'm not much for heights and the wind was mighty strong. But it offered a panorama of river and St. Paul skyline that was worth a little sweat and vertigo.

**MAKE A DAY OF IT:** Near Harriet Island Regional Park (200 Dr. Justus Ohage Boulevard; 651-266-6400), descend the stairs to Raspberry Island (1 Wabasha Street South), where the Minnesota Boat Club launches its rowing sculls. Try the scrumptious cannoli at Cossetta Italian Market and Pizzeria (211 West 7th Street; 651-222-3476) on West 7th and Chestnut streets.

# Mississippi Gorge Regional Park

Accessible from West River Parkway in Minneapolis and from
East River Parkway in St. Paul, between the Franklin Avenue
and Ford Parkway bridges • www.nps.gov/miss

**PRICE:** Free

**QUICK TIP:** Tackle the gorge in chunks: there's plenty to explore on
even a short hike

**RESTROOMS:** During the summer, portable toilets are available at
the parking areas along West River Parkway

**FAMILY TALK:** How did the river carve this gorge?

**MISSISSIPPI GORGE REGIONAL PARK** is a surprisingly wild stretch of ground along the river between Minneapolis and St. Paul. Steep cliffs and dense woods protect this narrow band of wilderness, the only gorge on the Mississippi River and home to foxes, eagles, turkeys, and beavers.

On a fall walk through the gorge, you can watch ducks and geese making their way south to the Gulf of Mexico, since the Mississippi is one of the nation's great flyways. The striation of limestone and sandstone becomes visible through the foliage at this time, too, and views of fall colors from the Lake Street and Ford Parkway bridges are breathtaking.

In winter, the gorge is a favorite snowshoe trail. The oak savanna restoration area just south of Lake Street, where 36th Street intersects West River Parkway, has hills, walking paths, and a hidden waterfall. North of Lake Street, just beyond the Minneapolis Rowing Club's boathouse, winter ice forms sheets down the cliff faces and animals suddenly cross your path.

West River Parkway also boasts a wide, paved, and well-maintained bike path, connecting the Midtown Greenway (p. 50) to Minnehaha Park (p. 28) and hugging the edge of the gorge. There are stairs and bike racks along the way, so you can lock up and explore the lower trails on foot.

Step a few feet off the trail here and you've walked a couple centuries into the past, when the river between Fort Snelling and St. Anthony Falls was entirely wild. Shielded by cliffs and trees, the gorge preserves time as much as it preserves nature.

**MAKE A DAY OF IT:** Rest up at Dunn Bros Coffee at 4648 East Lake Street (612-724-8647), or have a snack at Trotter's Café at 232 Cleveland Avenue North (651-645-8950).

# Washburn Park Water Tower

401 Prospect Avenue, Minneapolis, MN 55419
www.ci.minneapolis.mn.us

**PRICE:** Free

**QUICK TIP:** The tower has a habit of disappearing as you wind through the hills of Tangletown—look up!

**RESTROOMS:** Public restrooms are available at Fuller Park (4800 Grand Avenue South)

**FAMILY TALK:** Why are there knights encircling this tower?

**THOUGH IT LOOKS** more like a set piece for a Wagner opera, the massive concrete dome in the Tangletown neighborhood of Minneapolis is actually a water tower. Designed by architect Harry Wild Jones, who homesteaded in the neighborhood, the tower was completed in 1932.

The water tower is ringed by eight sculptures of helmeted knights resting on broadswords, with a giant stone eagle perched above each one. These knights are the "Guardians of Health," protecting the Minneapolis water supply from typhoid fever and other waterborne diseases. The eagles were modeled, or so Jones claimed, on an eagle that attacked him while he was clearing land for his nearby house.

Flight patterns at the Minneapolis–St. Paul International Airport now bring incoming jets low over the tower. They're a stunning sight, so close you can see the landing gear swoop down over the guardians' heads. The water tower's grassy hill is the perfect spot to lie back and watch the clouds—and planes— go by.

**MAKE A DAY OF IT:** Hike to the playground at Fuller Park (4800 Grand Avenue South; 612-370-4963), located at the foot of the Tangletown hill on Grand Avenue. Go further north on Grand to find Patisserie 46 (4552 Grand Avenue South; 612-354-3257), a French pastry shop, and Victor's 1959 Café (3756 Grand Avenue South; 612-827-8948), a Cuban restaurant serving fried sweet plantains.

# 37

# Twin City Model Railroad Museum

1021 Bandana Boulevard East, St. Paul, MN 55108
651-647-9628 • www.tcmrm.org

**PRICE:** $$

**QUICK TIP:** Models are decked out with miniature lights and decorations during the holidays; visit at night for the full effect

**RESTROOMS:** Plentiful

**FAMILY TALK:** How long do you think it took to build this display? Why do the short trains move faster than the long trains? What's underneath the table?

**THE PROBLEM WITH** the Twin City Model Railroad Museum is that it's simply too good. It will inspire you to design the best train layout you can fit in your basement and encourage your kids to pester you to make it better. But somewhere along the way, as you're trying to decipher the wiring diagrams that came with the tracks, you'll discover that good railroads aren't built in a day. By the time you figure out how to assemble all the pieces, the kids will be finding you a retirement home. And most retirement homes don't have room for model train layouts.

The museum will distract you from this dilemma soon enough, however, with its models of the Minneapolis milling district, a St. Paul neighborhood, and a detailed trestle bridge with tunnels and a river. Eventually, you'll accept that the museum's modelers are much better at this sort of thing than you'll ever be, and you'll commit to finding new wonders with each visit to their little world.

Bandana Square is an excellent location for the Model Railroad Museum, since it used to be the Northern Pacific Railway's St. Paul repair shop. There's an old steam locomotive parked out front, a wooden water tower, and a few boxcars and other train artifacts scattered around the grounds. If you look closely, you'll see where the big barn doors opened for cars and engines that needed repair inside the building.

Steel rails are still visible on the sidewalks, and if you walk through the complex's hotel, you'll see rails exposed in the hallway floors. The bellhops don't move luggage around by handcar, but that shouldn't stop young train enthusiasts from imagining cars and engines on the tracks.

**MAKE A DAY OF IT:** Check out the Jackson Street Roundhouse (p. 86) and Choo Choo Bob's Train Store (p. 84).

# 38

## Choo Choo Bob's Train Store

2050 Marshall Avenue, St. Paul, MN 55104
651-646-5252 • www.choochoobobs.com

**PRICE:** $$

**QUICK TIP:** There's parking in back, but the lot can be tight

**RESTROOMS:** Plentiful

**FAMILY TALK:** Why do people make model trains?

**CHOO CHOO BOB'S,** a train hobby store, is more than a place to be parted with your cash in exchange for HO model kits and LEGO train sets, though it certainly is that. It's also a round-house of train-related activities for young enthusiasts.

We first noticed the store shortly before it opened, when Jack and Peter were enamored of Thomas the Tank Engine. They learned their numbers and colors from Thomas, Edward, Percy, and others on the Island of Sodor. Soon they were moving on to more advanced train obsessions, including the model board in our basement. Every time we drove by Choo Choo Bob's, we'd slow down to see when the store would be opening.

When it did open, we found it was a convenient place to fill the gaps in the boys' train collection. The store also runs a regular train movie matinee at the Riverview Theater (3800 42nd Avenue South, Minneapolis, MN 55406; 612-729-7369; www.riverviewtheater.com), featuring clips of Thomas stories,

Johnny Cash songs, and Buster Keaton sketches put together in the kind of manic mishmash that only makes sense to kids.

Choo Choo Bob's sponsors field trips to train-related destinations beyond the Twin Cities. We took one to the St. Croix Railroad in Hudson, Wisconsin (325 South Cove Road, Hudson, WI 54016; 715-386-1871), where scaled-down trains just large enough to ride carry you through wooded terrain and over miniature trestle bridges. There's a trip to the Osceola & St. Croix Valley Railway (114 Depot Road, Osceola, WI 54020; 715-755-3570), as well. There, life-sized diesel and steam locomotives take riders for a forty-five minute trip.

**MAKE A DAY OF IT:** There's no shortage of treats nearby; choose from Izzy's Ice Cream Café (2034 Marshall Avenue; 651-603-1458), Sweets Bakeshop (2042 Marshall Avenue; 651-340-7138), and more.

# Jackson Street Roundhouse

193 Pennsylvania Avenue East, St. Paul, MN 55130
651-228-0263 • www.mtmuseum.org

**PRICE:** $$

**QUICK TIPS:** At Christmastime, the Jackson Street Roundhouse has one of the best Santas in the Twin Cities; bring the grandparents and make it a holiday outing

**RESTROOMS:** Plentiful

**FAMILY TALK:** How does a train turn around?

**THERE ARE PLENTY OF PLACES** in the region where you can ride a train. Most are short jaunts through a switchyard with a sing-along or a history lesson from the conductor. During their train phase, Jack and Peter were always excited to climb on board, but Kelly and I got a little jaded.

We expected Jackson Street Roundhouse to be more of the same. Little did we know that we'd get a chance to ride a turntable here as well as a train. The conductor on our ride had recently been certified to operate the giant platter that's used to turn trains around in the shop: during its heyday, a locomotive would be driven to the middle of the turntable, and then the huge circle would turn the engine to let it roll out in a different direction. It took very little arm-twisting to get the conductor to give us a spin. Later we explored the roundhouse's bunk cars, where railroad workers used to sleep; railroad signals, many still with flashing lights; and engines, several of which were being restored.

The turntable, shop equipment, and restoration projects at Jackson Street Roundhouse make it unique among the area's train-related stops. It offers a glimpse behind the curtain at the work that once went into operating steam engines and early diesels and at the work involved in restoring and maintaining them today. The romance of a lonely whistle in the distance wouldn't have been possible without shops like this one.

**MAKE A DAY OF IT:** Swede Hollow Park (615 7th Street East; 651-632-5111), across 35E from the Jackson Street Roundhouse, offers a glimpse into St. Paul's immigrant past and a great spot for a picnic and a stroll.

# Winter

# 40

# Holidazzle Parade

Runs along Nicollet Mall in downtown Minneapolis, from
12th Street to 4th Street, from just after Thanksgiving to just
before Christmas • 612-376-7669 • www.holidazzle.com

**PRICE:** Free

**QUICK TIP:** Spots in the skyway above Nicollet Mall fill up quickly—
get there early if you want a warm place to watch

**RESTROOMS:** Try the food court in Gaviidae Common (651 Nicollet
Mall)

**FAMILY TALK:** How many lights are on the costumes and floats?
How do the lights stay on?

**THE HOLIDAZZLE PARADE** down Nicollet Mall is an impressive theatrical and technological feat involving floats and costumes festooned with blinking lights. Professionals manage the
parade, but most of the people riding on the floats or walking
alongside them are volunteers.

The best view I've ever had of the Holidazzle was from right
in the middle of the parade, the year our family volunteered.
Jack and Peter were somewhat reluctantly dressed up as a giraffe
and an elephant to ride the circus train, while Kelly was Little
Red Riding Hood, with a flashing red basket and a sparkling cape.
I was cast as the Big Bad Wolf, one of the parade's arch villains.

Nicollet Mall is straight and wide, and the parade moves slowly, which made our adventure in volunteering a little easier. But my costume was hot and itchy. The battery pack that powered my lights was heavy, and the costume's glowing teeth made looking out of the wolf's mouth difficult. I navigated mostly by the sound of boos and hisses directed at me. I lurched down the avenue, stumbling into the crowd only a few times, which merely enhanced my villainy.

The skyways across Nicollet Mall probably offer better views of the parade's lights, storybook characters, and holiday floats. The sidewalk isn't bad either, if you don't mind costumed wolves tripping into you. However, nothing gets you into the holiday spirit quite like scaring kids and howling at skyways with your terrible teeth flashing in the dark.

**MAKE A DAY OF IT:** Do your holiday shopping along Nicollet Mall and marvel at the Macy's holiday display, located in the store's upstairs auditorium (700 Nicollet Avenue; 612-375-2200).

# 41

# Minnesota Center for Book Arts

1011 Washington Avenue South, Minneapolis, MN 55415
612-215-2520 • www.mnbookarts.org

**PRICE:** Free (fees for classes and workshops)

**QUICK TIP:** Have the kids search for the building's book-inspired details, such as the pages in the staircase banister

**RESTROOMS:** Plentiful

**FAMILY TALK:** What kinds of materials are used to make books? Do you like books with or without pictures?

**BY THE TIME JACK AND PETER** are my age, the book as a physical object may seem old-fashioned. But no e-book can do with pixels and plastic what the craftspeople at the Minnesota Center for Book Arts (MCBA) can do with paper and ink.

MCBA is part of the Open Book complex, which also houses the Loft Literary Center and Milkweed Editions, making it an exciting hub for the written, printed, and painted word. All parts of the production process are celebrated here, from pulling words out of the author's mind to putting them between fascinating covers.

The Open Book gallery displays books re-imagined as pieces of art. We've seen books printed on paper, wood, and stone, hung on walls, disassembled into loose pages, and bound into intricate boxes. The center's shop contains all sorts of supplies and inspiration for would-be book builders. And MCBA runs classes and workshops for all ages on printing, assembling, and creating pages and pictures and words.

**MAKE A DAY OF IT:** Plan ahead to catch a reading or a book signing at the building's coffee shop. Wander across Washington Avenue to explore Gold Medal Park (p. 42).

# 42

# Bakken Museum

3537 Zenith Avenue South, Minneapolis, MN 55416
612-926-3878 • www.thebakken.org

**PRICE:** $$$

**QUICK TIPS:** Take advantage of the museum's hands-on
exhibits, including the giant magnets in the lower-level gallery;
the Frankenstein exhibit is great but best for older kids

**RESTROOMS:** Plentiful

**FAMILY TALK:** Why do some sparks sting more than others?
What materials carry electricity well? Why is there a Frankenstein
exhibit here?

**YESTERDAY'S SCIENCE FICTION** often becomes today's sci-
ence, tamed down a bit. We're not flying Jetsons' space cars, but
we can drive fuel-efficient hybrids. We may not see Captain Nemo
submarines battling giant squid, but modern underwater robots
are exploring ocean valleys. And although shambling monsters
aren't being brought to life by bolts of lightning, human hearts are
kept beating by tiny tickers embedded in the chest.

The Bakken Museum is a place where science fiction and
science intersect: Mary Shelley's Victor Frankenstein is said to
have inspired real-life electrical engineer Earl Bakken, the muse-
um's namesake, to create a transistorized pacemaker that saves
lives. On a stormy day, the museum's stately Tudor mansion

looks a bit like Frankenstein's castle, but most of the exhibits inside owe more to the Age of Reason than to monster movies.

The Electricity Party Room lets kids play with static electricity to ring bells and shoot sparks; there's the risk of a small shock, but that only makes the science more fun. The Mindball game—in which you levitate and move a Ping-Pong ball by controlling your brain waves—is especially satisfying. You win by relaxing, sending long beta waves of tranquility to crush your overwrought opponent. At last, I've found a game where the patience that the boys have forced me to learn lets me beat them every time.

**MAKE A DAY OF IT:** Organize a technology double-header: the Bakken Museum in the morning, followed by the Pavek Museum of Broadcasting (p. 16) in St. Louis Park that afternoon.

# 43

## Sledding at Minnehaha Creek

Above Minnehaha Creek at Cedar Avenue in Minneapolis

**PRICE:** Free

**QUICK TIPS:** The slope on the east side of the creek tends to be steep and icy; head to the west side for a gentler ride

**RESTROOMS:** Try the nearby Caribou Coffee (4745 Cedar Avenue South)

**FAMILY TALK:** Why is a sled faster on the snow than it is on the grass?

**FOR A LANDSCAPE** that seems so uniformly flat, the Twin Cities has a surprising number of top-notch sledding hills. In St. Paul, the slopes behind the Highland Park Water Tower (p. 74) make for speedy downhill swooshes. Our favorite sledding spot is in Minneapolis above Minnehaha Creek at Cedar Avenue. It's a nice wide slope with a variety of inclines, including an icy bump that sends lightweight sledders into the air.

One year after Christmas, we hit the hill and were joined by a local television news crew. The reporters tried to get a few words from Jack and Peter about their technique, but the boys had no interest in securing their fifteen minutes of fame. They were focused on the hill, like a couple of surfers waiting for the big wave. Nonsledders just don't understand the discipline that goes into a good ride.

The hill doesn't have to be big to inspire. Even the tiny slope in our front yard can support hours of after-school sledding. My best efforts at sidewalk shoveling are often quickly undone by flying saucers and belly flops. The city really should give leeway to residents shoveling sidewalks that border an active sledding hill.

**MAKE A DAY OF IT:** Bring your snowshoes and cross-country skis for hours more fun on the frozen creek, then warm up at Nokomis Beach Coffee (4956 28th Avenue South; 612-729-2190).

# 44

# Skiing at Hyland and Buck Hill

**Hyland Ski & Snowboard Area:** 8800 Chalet Road, Bloomington, MN 55438; 763-694-7800 • www.threeriversparks.org

**Buck Hill:** 15400 Buck Hill Road, Burnsville, MN 55306 952-435-7174 • www.buckhill.com

**PRICE:** $

**QUICK TIP:** Don't forget the sunscreen! When sunlight reflects off the snow, it can cause sunburn

**RESTROOMS:** Plentiful

**FAMILY TALK:** Which is faster, a sled or skis? Is it easier to ski with or without poles? How high is the chair lift?

**SKIING IS ONE OF THOSE SKILLS** that's best taught by someone other than your parents. That was certainly the case for me. My father tried to teach me to ski years ago on a Boy Scout trip and finally handed me off to another dad. That man wasn't much more successful but at least he didn't generate as much angst. When the boys expressed an interest in skiing, Kelly and I didn't even consider trying to teach them ourselves. The professionals at Hyland Ski & Snowboard Area in Bloomington know better how to connect kids with their skis.

The boys' ski instructor was closer to their age than mine and full of youthful enthusiasm. He not only had slope skills to pass along but also knew silly songs and jokes that the boys repeated for weeks. Very soon after strapping on their boots and skis, they were up the chairlift to more challenging hills. Meanwhile, I endangered other peoples' children on the bunny hill, amazed that skis seem so much faster now than they did when I was twelve.

Since the boys' initial lessons at Hyland, we've also tried out Burnsville's Buck Hill, which boasts a slightly more challenging beginners' hill for me and a higher chairlift for the boys. When Jack and Peter master the Twin Cities hills, there are more impressive slopes farther north to challenge them. I'm hoping those hills have comfortable lodges and big windows, so I can admire their skiing from a level spot.

**MAKE A DAY OF IT:** From Buck Hill, it's a quick drive to the Minnesota Zoo (p. 8), where you can view more snow, and animals, from the warmth of the monorail.

# 45

# Minnesota State Capitol

75 Rev. Dr. Martin Luther King Jr. Boulevard, St. Paul, MN
55155; 651-296-2881 • www.mnhs.org/places/sites/msc

**PRICE:** Free

**QUICK TIPS:** Check online for special events; go when the state
legislature is in session for an especially educational time

**RESTROOMS:** Plentiful

**FAMILY TALK:** Why does the Capitol have a dome? How many
people can sit inside the legislative chamber?

**THERE ARE A HUNDRED WAYS** to approach the Minnesota State Capitol. Politically, it's where the state's lawmakers
and governors have met since 1905. Architecturally, it's Cass
Gilbert's masterpiece. And artistically, the building and grounds
are packed with paintings, statues, and frescoes commemorat-
ing veterans, wars, governors, and legislators. History is the lens
through which I see most things, and at the Capitol traces of the
Civil War and the rise of Prohibition are particularly evident.

Veterans of the Civil War shaped state government when
they returned home from battle. Most of Minnesota's governors from 1866 to 1900 were veterans, and the Capitol is still a
showcase for that generation's role in saving the Union. Statues
of Civil War leaders ring the second-floor balcony beneath the
building's great classical dome, and of the six paintings in the

Governor's Reception Room, four depict Civil War battle scenes. The most impressive painting is Howard Pyle's *The Battle of Nashville*; if you have a collection of Civil War books, at least one of them likely uses this dramatic painting on its cover.

Hidden away beneath the Capitol is the Rathskeller, a cafeteria adorned with intricate frescoes and German drinking doggerel such as *"Ein frischer Trank, der Arbeit Dank"* ("Enjoy a glass after a duty well performed"). The Rathskeller came under scrutiny following World War I and during Prohibition, when such phrases were painted over. The room was restored to its former glory about ten years ago and now makes for a charming place to eat and relax, although it is open only when the legislature is in session. With high windows and bright walls, it doesn't feel like a basement at all. Perhaps if there were some Paulaner or Hacker-Pschorr on tap to go along with the poems on the walls, state government would run with a bit more ease.

**MAKE A DAY OF IT:** Learn more about state government and politics at the Minnesota History Center (p. 52) down the street and at the St. Paul Central Library (p. 12) down the hill.

# 46

# Bell Museum of Natural History

10 Church Street Southeast, Minneapolis, MN 55455
612-624-7083 • www.bellmuseum.org

**PRICE:** $$

**QUICK TIP:** Parking is available in area ramps, but may be limited
during special events

**RESTROOMS:** Plentiful but not all wheelchair accessible

**FAMILY TALK:** Why do the pelts have different textures?
How do the plants and animals in each habitat work together?

**FOUNDED IN 1872** as a University of Minnesota research facil-
ity, the Bell Museum holds detailed dioramas of North American
animals in their natural habitats. The museum gives visitors a
close-up look at moose, beaver, loons, and bear. These are views
my kids and I would never get, nor likely dare to get, in the wild.

In the Touch and See Room, the displays not only stand still
but also invite little hands to explore. You can pet a stuffed griz-
zly bear, compare fox, lynx, and beaver pelts, and pick up horns
and antlers. The moose rack, in particular, drew the attention
of Jack and Peter, who have been obsessed with the king of the
north woods ever since we spotted one in New Hampshire. It
took both of them to heft the moose antlers at the Bell, giving
them a new respect for this awesome and usually shy giant.
The Touch and See Room also contains glass cages of things you

may not want to touch, including snakes, centipedes, and giant cockroaches.

Near the museum entrance is a small gallery dedicated to the history and practice of the museum. It includes a diorama in progress, tools of the taxidermists and artists who built the displays, and answers to a few of the questions kids are likely to ask during a visit. This room is worth two stops: one on the way in as an introduction and inoculation against the bad information dads sometimes offer up, and one on the way out as a reminder of the effort that goes into constructing such lifelike and detailed habitats.

**MAKE A DAY OF IT:** Drive to the Prospect Park Water Tower (p. 18) for treetop views of city habitats.

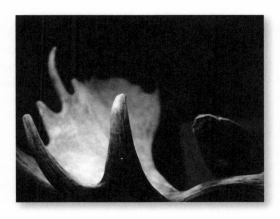

# 47

# Rice Park

109 West 4th Street, St. Paul, MN 55102 • www.stpaul.gov

**PRICE:** Free

**QUICK TIP:** Watch the St. Paul Winter Carnival (p. 106) website for details on when artists are carving blocks of ice at the park

**RESTROOMS:** Head indoors to the St. Paul Central Library (p. 14)

**FAMILY TALK:** Why are there statues of Peanuts characters here?

**THE POLICE CHIEF** of Memphis, Tennessee, donated a pair of squirrels to Rice Park in 1873, or so says the park's historical marker. This has always struck me as strange: Why Memphis? Why squirrels? Why Rice Park? Unfortunately, the marker is silent on the important issues. It merely mentions the squirrels and moves on, forcing the reader to speculate. Luckily, the benches at Rice Park are an ideal spot to sit and think.

If those squirrels' descendents live on in the park's trees and bushes, they must be grateful to their Memphis benefactor. They've got one of the nicest homes in the Twin Cities. There's a fountain, and lush and shady grassy areas to enjoy in summer. With the hum of traffic around it and people strolling through it, Rice Park has the feel of an old-world plaza. It's a public space not set apart from the city but firmly embedded in it.

In winter, Rice Park is an icy hotspot. During the St. Paul Winter Carnival (p. 106), artists carve beauty from blocks of ice in the park. There's a small ice rink nearby, too, with inexpensive skate rentals and free skating. It may not be Central Park, but Rice Park holds a good deal more romance than the standard city park.

**MAKE A DAY OF IT:** Loop around the park and admire four of St. Paul's most impressive buildings: the library (p. 12), Ordway Center for the Performing Arts (345 Washington Street; 651-282-3000), Landmark Center (75 West 5th Street; 651-292-3233), and St. Paul Hotel (350 Market Street; 651-292-9292).

# 48

# St. Paul Winter Carnival

Events occur throughout St. Paul during the last week of January and the first week of February • www.winter-carnival.com

**PRICE:** $

**QUICK TIP:** Use the Treasure Hunt for the Medallion to teach your kids about St. Paul geography and history

**RESTROOMS:** Plentiful

**FAMILY TALK:** Why is there a carnival in the winter? How do they shape the ice sculptures?

**THERE ARE ONLY TWO SANE WAYS** to cope with a Minnesota winter. You can lock yourself inside with a pot of coffee and a stack of books. Or you can defiantly embrace the cold. The St. Paul Winter Carnival decidedly adopts the latter strategy. It's an icy Mardi Gras, a saturnalian rebellion against Old Man Winter's chilly clutches.

Not much has changed at the Winter Carnival since F. Scott Fitzgerald's "The Ice Palace," a fictional account of the cold-weather festival. While you're discouraged now from riding on sleds behind cars down St. Paul's snowy streets, there are still roasted chestnuts and torchlight parades. Locals dressed in costume bring to life the raucous, if sometimes raunchy, exploits of the Vulcans and Klondike Kate. The carnival has an old-fashioned feel. It's not staid and quaint but wild and slightly dangerous, like the old-time river town that lies just below the surface of modern-day St. Paul.

The ice sculptures at Rice Park are the boys' favorite part of the carnival, and they're a pleasure best enjoyed cold. The ideal years are those when the mercury dips below zero and the sun hides behind the clouds, keeping the sculptures' fragile beauty pristine for the duration.

Even better than seeing a finished ice sculpture is watching one in progress. Creating one of these chilly fantasies involves ice picks, chain saws, blowtorches, and buckets of hot water. Jack and Peter would love to be able to use these tools for their own creations and can't quite understand why they're only allowed to use snow shovels and mittens.

Hot chocolate at the St. Paul Hotel (350 Market Street; 651-292-9292) and a gold souvenir coin from a carnival dignitary round out any carnival visit.

**MAKE A DAY OF IT:** The St. Paul Grill (350 Market Street; 651-224-7455) makes for a special-occasion meal that older kids will appreciate; Anita's Café in the Landmark Center (75 West 5th Street; 651-292-4160) is a casual place with kid-friendly offerings; and any visit to downtown St. Paul is greatly enhanced by a stop at the Science Museum of Minnesota (p. 24) or the Children's Museum (p. 22).

# 49

## Snowshoeing at Mississippi Gorge Regional Park

Accessible from West River Parkway in Minneapolis and from East River Parkway in St. Paul, between the Franklin Avenue and Ford Parkway bridges • www.nps.gov/miss

**PRICE:** Free

**QUICK TIP:** Make sure your snowshoes will fit over your warmest boots before you leave the store

**RESTROOMS:** Try the Riverview Café (3745 42nd Avenue South, Minneapolis) or the Dunn Brothers Coffee Shop (4648 East Lake Street, Minneapolis); there are no portable toilets available during the winter

**FAMILY TALK:** How does a snowshoe keep you on top of the snow? What animals have feet that work like snowshoes?

**IF YOU CAN WALK,** you can snowshoe. We started the boys on cheap plastic Spider-Man snowshoes when they were four years old. Our first trips were just around the block, climbing the mountains of ice and scree pushed up by the snowplows, but we quickly graduated to the Mississippi River gorge. With crusty snow filling up the spaces around the trees in the oak savanna restoration area, the gorge encouraged us to become arctic explorers tracking raccoon, foxes, and squirrels.

At Cub Scout camp, I always lead a snowshoe hike with a group of galumphing scouts, many of whom are trying out snowshoes for the first time. We look for woodland creatures and get up close to woods that are overgrown and unreachable in the spring and summer. Last year I was especially impressed with one of the youngest kids in the pack, who pressed on with tenacity and enthusiasm despite far-too-big shoes that made him trip over himself every few yards.

Since they aren't built for speed, snowshoes are also a great way to keep a gang of young hikers together. On a normal walk in the woods, I would have to work hard to keep everyone in sight and rein them in when they get too far ahead. On snowshoes, I catch up to the vanguards as they fall down. If they do move out of sight, it's not hard to track them down. Even little feet leave big impressions in the snow.

**MAKE A DAY OF IT:** Reward your arctic explorers with a hot chocolate at one of the nearby coffee shops on the Minneapolis side (Riverview Café, 3745 42nd Avenue South, 612-722-7234; Dunn Brothers, 4648 East Lake Street, 612-724-8647; Blue Moon Café, 3822 East Lake Street, 612-721-9230; Fireroast Mountain Café, 3800 37th Avenue South, 612-724-9895); or take in a movie at the Riverview Theater (3800 42nd Avenue, Minneapolis; 612-729-7369), a classic single-screen venue that frequently shows kid movie matinees.

# 50

## Skating in the Parks

The cities of Minneapolis and St. Paul open outdoor ice rinks
in December; rinks are typically open through February;
www.minneapolisparks.org • www.stpaul.gov

**PRICE:** Free

**QUICK TIPS:** Most parks have skates you can borrow for free; check
park websites for rink and warming house hours

**RESTROOMS:** Public restrooms are available in most park buildings
and are often accessible directly from the warming rooms

**FAMILY TALK:** What makes ice so slippery?

**MY WIFE KELLY** was born in Canada. This is seldom an issue.
Apart from eating french fries with vinegar and opening paper-
crown crackers at Christmas, Canadians are a lot like Americans.
Except when it comes to skating.

When the boys turned four, Kelly fitted them with skates
and sent them out on the ice. Predictably, they landed on their
rumps and started to shriek. Kelly picked them back up and set
them on their skates, and down they went again, with yet more
defiant shrieks.

That was how their first half-dozen skating lessons went.
Strangers offered us walkers, standing sleds, and folding
chairs—all devices that other kids at the rinks were using to
stay upright. But my wife politely declined all assistance. Her

philosophy is that you learn to skate by learning to fall. And it's best to get the hard lessons out of the way early.

Miraculously, on what I expected to be a seventh awful experience on the ice, Jack and Peter started to skate. Not well, not fast, and not without falling, but there was clearly more skating than flailing. Kelly gave me her proud "I told you so" look and skated away, backwards, to start their next lesson.

Now every November our family starts watching the neighborhood baseball fields, waiting for the wooden barriers to go up and the hoses to come out to flood the diamonds. The boys fearlessly swoop down icy hills onto the rinks while I carefully sidestep down the stairs, leaning on a hockey stick that I use more for balance than puck-handling. They try to race me, but I don't stand a chance. I'm far too nervous about taking a tumble. They got all of their falling out of the way at the start and now have nothing ahead of them but gliding.

**MAKE A DAY OF IT:** Skating and cocoa go together well—enjoy a hot chocolate at one of the many local coffee shops.

# 51

# Conservatory at Como Park

1225 Estabrook Drive, St. Paul, MN 55103
651-487-8200 • www.comozooconservatory.org

**PRICE:** $

**QUICK TIP:** See the conservatory gardens in all their splendor during the seasonal flower shows

**RESTROOMS:** Plentiful

**FAMILY TALK:** Where did these plants come from? How is the air in the conservatory different from the air outside?

**THE MARJORIE MCNEELY CONSERVATORY** at Como Park is a magical bubble of spring that stays warm and green even when the rest of the Twin Cities is besieged by winter. Step through the glass doors into the conservatory's tropical humidity and you'll see exotic trees, babbling fountains, and stone nymphs cavorting among the flowers. A visit to the conservatory is a sure, if brief, cure for the winter blues.

As magical as the place is in the winter, we like it better in the fall. There's enough of a chill in the air to appreciate the sunken garden's warmth, but you also can roam around the Japanese garden outside and take in its vibrant colors against the stone lanterns and bridges. Koi swim in the pools, and there are narrow walkways to navigate. Everyone can use bigger voices than are normally allowed in closed, inside spaces.

When the Japanese garden is covered in snow, Jack and Peter turn to the indoor bonsai displays. These are real trees, not dwarfs, that have been carefully cultivated into miniature versions of themselves. The boys are fascinated by the tiny rocks that replicate a windswept mountainside and the decorative pots that hold the trees. They've pointed out that our own hydrangea tree, which has stubbornly refused to grow and bloom for five years, might count as a bonsai, but I attribute its failure to inattention rather than careful pruning.

**MAKE A DAY OF IT:** Visit the cold-weather-loving animals at the Como Zoo (p. 72).

# 52

## Minneapolis Institute of Arts

2400 3rd Avenue South, Minneapolis, MN 55404
612- 870-3000 • www.artsmia.org

**PRICE:** $

**QUICK TIP:** Don't miss the museum's American and European period rooms, which are decorated for the holiday season

**RESTROOMS:** Plentiful

**FAMILY TALK:** What are the picture frames made of? If you put different paintings and statues together, would that change how you see them?

**I HAVE A FEW OLD FRIENDS** I like to visit at the Minneapolis Institute of Arts: the veiled lady, N.C. Wyeth's Cream of Wheat cowboys, and the giant face of Frank. The boys have an old friend they like to visit, too, but it's not a work of art. Rather, it's the gilded elevator cage in the back galleries.

There are paintings and statues they like, too, of course. The tornado over St. Paul is a favorite, and they find the reproductions of historic rooms fascinating. But the elevator and other parts of the physical structure—staircases, landings, windows, and doors—seem to them as much a part of the art experience as the things hanging on walls.

At first, I balked at this. I wanted them to admire the brushstrokes, the use of light, the compositions and angles in my favorite pieces. They should at least admire the Chinese jade mountains and temple statues. But there was no point in swimming against this particular tide. Engineering is an art, too, and deserving of appreciation.

Seeing the Institute through my little engineers' eyes gave me an interesting perspective on how a museum works. How do they hang such heavy paintings? What sort of ladder must you use to get to the top of the Polynesian ancestor poles? Working from this how-do-they-do-it perspective led to some interesting discussions—and has made me enjoy my visits even more.

**MAKE A DAY OF IT:** Attend a play at the Children's Theatre Company (2400 3rd Avenue South; 612-874-0400)—your kids may be inspired by their peers on stage. Check out the work of up-and-coming artists at the MCAD Gallery (2501 Stevens Avenue; 612-874-3667), south of the MIA.

# Index

## A

amusement parks: Como Town Amusement Park, 40–41; Minnesota State Fair, 58–59

animals: Bell Museum of Natural History, 102–3; Como Park Zoo, 72–73; Minnesota Zoo, 8–9

athletic activities: Chain of Lakes, 34–35; Clifton E. French Regional Park, 64–65; Gold Medal Park, 42–43; ice skating in parks, 110–11; Jim Lupient Water Park, 56–57; Midtown Greenway, 50–51; Mississippi River Visitor Center and Walking Tour, 76–77; 9 Nights of Music, 54–55; St. Paul Saints Baseball, 46–47; skiing at Hyland and Buck Hill, 98–99; sledding at Minnehaha Creek, 96–97; snowshoeing at Mississippi Gorge Regional Park, 108–9

## B

Bakken Museum, 94–95
Bell Museum of Natural History, 102–3
Big Back Yard, 26–27
Buck Hill, 98–99

## C

Chain of Lakes, 34–35
Choo Choo Bob's Train Store, 84–85
Clifton E. French Regional Park, 64–65
Como Park Zoo, 72–73
Como Town Amusement Park, 40–41
Conservatory at Como Park, 112–13

# D

Dowling Community Garden, 10–11
Dylan, Bob, 18


# E

educational activities: Bakken Museum, 94–95; Bell Museum of Natural
    History, 102–3; Big Back Yard, 26–27; Como Park Zoo, 72–73; farmers
    markets, 30–31; Lock and Dam No. 1, 48–49; Mill City Museum, 36–37;
    Minneapolis Central Library, 12–13; Minneapolis Institute of Arts,
    114–15; Minnesota Center for Book Arts, 92–93; Minnesota Children's
    Museum, 22–23; Minnesota History Center, 52–53; Minnesota State
    Capitol, 100–101; Minnesota Zoo, 8–9; Mississippi River Visitor Center
    and Walking Tour, 76–77; Pavek Museum of Broadcasting, 16–17;
    St. Paul Central Library, 14–15; Science Museum of Minnesota, 24–25;
    Steamboat *Minnehaha,* 38–39; Walker Art Center and Minneapolis
    Sculpture Garden, 62–63


# F

farmers markets, 30–31. *See also* markets
Foshay, Wilbur, 66–67
Foshay Tower, 66–67
free activities: Como Park Zoo, 72–73; Dowling Community Garden,
    10–11; Gold Medal Park, 42–43; In the Heart of the Beast MayDay
    Parade, 6–7; Highland Park Water Tower, 74–75; Holidazzle Parade,
    90–91; ice skating in parks, 110–11; Midtown Greenway, 50–51; Mil-
    waukee Avenue, 20–21; Minneapolis Central Library, 12–13; Minne-
    apolis Sculpture Garden, 62–63; Minnehaha Falls, 28–29; Minnesota
    Center for Book Arts, 92–93; Minnesota State Capitol, 100–101; Mis-
    sissippi Gorge Regional Park, 78–79; Mississippi River Visitor Center
    and Walking Tour, 76–77; 9 Nights of Music, 54–55; Prospect Park
    Water Tower, 18–19; Rice Park, 104–5; St. Paul Central Library, 14–15;
    sledding at Minnehaha Creek, 96–97; snowshoeing at Mississippi
    Gorge Regional Park, 108–9; Stone Arch Bridge, 44–45; Washburn
    Park Water Tower, 80–81

## G

gardens. *See* parks and gardens
Gilbert, Cass, 100
Gold Medal Park, 42–43

## H

Hendrix, Jimi, 18
Highland Park Water Tower, 74–75
historical sites: Dowling Community Garden, 10–11; Foshay Tower,
    66–67; Highland Park Water Tower, 74–75; Lock and Dam No. 1,
    48–49; Midtown Global Market, 70–71; Mill City Museum, 36–37;
    Milwaukee Avenue, 20–21; Minnehaha Falls, 28–29; Minnesota State
    Capitol, 100–101; Mississippi River Visitor Center and Walking Tour,
    76–77; Prospect Park Water Tower, 18–19; Steamboat *Minnehaha,*
    38–39; Stone Arch Bridge, 44–45; Washburn Park Water Tower, 80–81
Hmongtown Marketplace, 68–69
Holidazzle Parade, 90–91
Hyland Ski & Snowboard Area, 98–99

## I

ice skating, 110–11
indoor activities: Bakken Museum, 94–95; Bell Museum of Natural His-
    tory, 102–3; Choo Choo Bob's Train Store, 84–85; Conservatory at
    Como Park, 112–13; Foshay Tower, 66–67; Jackson Street Roundhouse,
    86–87; Midtown Global Market, 70–71; Mill City Museum, 36–37;
    Minneapolis Central Library, 12–13; Minneapolis Institute of Arts,
    114–15; Minnesota Center for Book Arts, 92–93; Minnesota Children's
    Museum, 22–23; Minnesota History Center, 52–53; Minnesota State
    Capitol, 100–101; Pavek Museum of Broadcasting, 16–17; St. Paul Cen-
    tral Library, 14–15; Science Museum of Minnesota, 24–25; Twin City
    Model Railroad Museum, 82–83; Walker Art Center, 62–63
In the Heart of the Beast MayDay Parade, 6–7
In the Heart of the Beast Puppet and Mask Theatre, 6–7

# J

Jackson Street Roundhouse, 86–87
Jim Lupient Water Park, 56–57
Jones, Harry Wild, 80

# L

libraries: Minneapolis Central Library, 12–13; St. Paul Central Library,
    14–15
Lock and Dam No. 1, 48–49
Longfellow, Henry Wadsworth, 28

# M

markets: farmers markets, 30–31; Hmongtown Marketplace, 68–69;
    Midtown Global Market, 70–71
McCloskey, Robert, 14
Midtown Farmers Market, 30–31
Midtown Global Market, 70–71
Midtown Greenway, 50–51
Mill City Farmers Market, 30–31
Mill City Museum, 36–37
Mill Ruins Park, 37
Milwaukee Avenue, 20–21
Minneapolis Central Library, 12–13
Minneapolis Farmers Market, 30–31
Minneapolis Institute of Arts, 114–15
Minnehaha Creek, sledding at, 96–97
Minnehaha Falls, 28–29
Minnehaha Park, 28–29
Minnesota Center for Book Arts, 92–93
Minnesota Children's Museum, 22–23
Minnesota History Center, 52–53
Minnesota State Capitol, 100–101
Minnesota State Fair, 58–59
Minnesota Zoo, 8–9

Mississippi Gorge Regional Park, 78–79, 108–9
Mississippi River Visitor Center and Walking Tour, 76–77
model trains, 82–85
museums: Bakken Museum, 94–95; Bell Museum of Natural History,
102–3; Foshay Tower, 66–67; Mill City Museum, 36–37; Minneapolis
Institute of Arts, 114–15; Minnesota Center for Book Arts, 92–93;
Minnesota Children's Museum, 22–23; Minnesota History Center,
52–53; Pavek Museum of Broadcasting, 16–17; Science Museum of
Minnesota, 24–25; Twin City Model Railroad Museum, 82–83; Walker
Art Center and Minneapolis Sculpture Garden, 62–63

## N
9 Nights of Music, 54–55

## O
outdoor activities: Big Back Yard, 26–27; Chain of Lakes, 34–35; Clifton
E. French Regional Park, 64–65; Como Park Zoo, 72–73; Como Town
Amusement Park, 40–41; Dowling Community Garden, 10–11; farmers
markets, 30–31; Gold Medal Park, 42–43; In the Heart of the Beast
MayDay Parade, 6–7; Highland Park Water Tower, 74–75; Hmongtown
Marketplace, 68–69; Holidazzle Parade, 90–91; ice skating in parks,
110–11; Jim Lupient Water Park, 56–57; Midtown Greenway, 50–51;
Milwaukee Avenue, 20–21; Minneapolis Sculpture Garden, 62–63;
Minnehaha Falls, 28–29; Minnesota State Fair, 58–59; Minnesota Zoo,
8–9; Mississippi Gorge Regional Park, 78–79; Mississippi River Visitor
Center and Walking Tour, 76–77; 9 Nights of Music, 54–55; Prospect
Park Water Tower, 18–19; Rice Park, 104–5; St. Paul Saints Baseball,
46–47; St. Paul Winter Carnival, 106–7; skiing at Hyland and Buck Hill,
98–99; sledding at Minnehaha Creek, 96–97; snowshoeing at Missis-
sippi Gorge Regional Park, 108–9; Steamboat *Minnehaha*, 38–39; Stone
Arch Bridge, 44–45; Washburn Park Water Tower, 80–81

## P

parades: In the Heart of the Beast MayDay Parade, 6–7; Holidazzle
    Parade, 90–91
parks and gardens: Clifton E. French Regional Park, 64–65; Conserva-
    tory at Como Park, 112–13; Dowling Community Garden, 10–11; Gold
    Medal Park, 42–43; ice skating in, 110–11; Mississippi Gorge Regional
    Park, 78–79; Rice Park, 104–5; Walker Art Center and Minneapolis
    Sculpture Garden, 62–63; Washburn Park Water Tower, 80–81
Pavek, Joe, 16
Pavek Museum of Broadcasting, 16–17
Prospect Park Water Tower, 18–19
Pyle, Howard, 101


## R

Rathskeller cafeteria, 101
Rice Park, 104–5


## S

St. Paul Central Library, 14–15
St. Paul Farmers' Market, 30–31
St. Paul Saints Baseball, 46–47
St. Paul Winter Carnival, 106–7
scenic sites: Chain of Lakes, 34–35; Foshay Tower, 66–67; Highland Park
    Water Tower, 74–75; Milwaukee Avenue, 20–21; Minnehaha Falls,
    28–29; Mississippi Gorge Regional Park, 78–79; Mississippi River
    Visitor Center and Walking Tour, 76–77; Prospect Park Water Tower,
    18–19; Rice Park, 104–5; Steamboat *Minnehaha*, 38–39
Science Museum of Minnesota, 24–25
skating, in parks, 110–11
skiing, at Hyland and Buck Hill, 98–99
sledding, at Minnehaha Creek, 96–97
snowshoeing, at Mississippi Gorge Regional Park, 108–9
Steamboat *Minnehaha*, 38–39
Stone Arch Bridge, 44–45

**T**

trains, 82–87
Twin City Model Railroad Museum, 82–83


**W**

Walker Art Center and Minneapolis Sculpture Garden, 62–63
Washburn Park Water Tower, 80–81
Water Park, Jim Lupient, 56–57
Wigington, Clarence W., 74


**Z**

zoos: Como Park Zoo, 72–73; Minnesota Zoo, 8–9

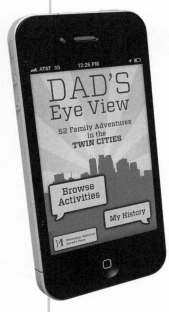

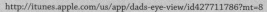